# HOW TO DRAW DRAGONS AND OTHER MYTHICAL CREATURES

## EMMETT ELVIN

Kandour Ltd

Published by
Kandour Limited
Monticello House
45 Russell Square
London WC1B 4JP
United Kingdom

First published 2007

10 9 8 7 6 5 4 3 2 1

Author: Emmett Elvin

Jacket Design and Layout: Emmett Elvin

Production: Carol Titchener & Karen Lomax

Additional Material: Kaspa Hazlewood

Printed and bound in China

ISBN-13: 978-1-905741-87-8

A catalogue record of this book is available from the British Library

# CONTENTS

# FOREWORD

What's fifty feet long, covered in scales and can burn you to a crisp?

Okay, okay, you may be thinking of a giant goldfish armed with a blowtorch, but I doubt it. Chances are the first thing that came into your head was a dragon.

Tyrannosaurus may be king of the dinosaurs, the lion may be king of the jungle. There is only one choice for the undisputed, hands-down ruler of all mythical creatures: the dragon.

Down through the centuries this most elemental of beasts has haunted the imaginations of cultures throughout the world. Although they may differ in appearance and size the essence of what a dragon represents remains consistent wherever on the globe this magical creature is found.

This book is an exploration of these various forms and an attempt to show how anyone with enthusiasm for the task can draw dragons. Every step of the way is presented with total clarity, taking the bewilderment out of the task and showing that great complexity begins with the utmost simplicity.

Also packed into these pages are a host of other popular mythical creatures: the Medusa, the Chimera, The Unicorn and many more are laid bare in their construction, waiting only for you to sharpen a pencil and unleash your own mythical masterpieces on the world. It's easy when you know how, and this book will show you how!

For the beginners among you I've prepared a special primer section in the introduction. For the more experienced, just dive in at whatever point takes your fancy.

Emmett Elvin  December 2005

# INTRODUCTION

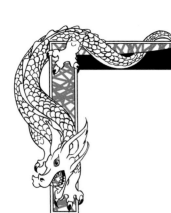 

# INTRODUCTION

DRAGONS!

Of all the creatures we could choose to draw, whether real or fantastic, dragons are among the toughest. They typically contain elements of several creature types and are usually lavishly decorated. As such they present a unique challenge to our drawing skills.

Dragons draw on characteristics of some of the world's most powerful beasts and top these off with wild whiskers, amazing armor-plating and mesmerizing mantles. They represent the embodiment of mankind's wonder and fear of the natural world. They are the most awesome, the most frightening and the most distinctive monsters to be spawned by the human imagination.

The purpose of this introduction is to give you an understanding of how all mythical creatures are constructed, ultimately allowing you to give free rein to your imagination. Trying to draw a full-blown winged dragon before we've examined the basic elements of creature construction will most likely end in frustration.

First we need to look at how simpler creatures are constructed and gain confidence in our ability to have complete control over these.

## STOP MAKING MISTAKES!

If there's one thing that separates professional artists from amateurs it's something called *planning*.

Planning can really bore the pants off people who want instant results and can't wait to begin producing masterpieces.

The point of this introduction therefore is to demonstrate how any creature you care to draw is constructed from the ground up. This means starting with just the simplest one or two lines and only adding more detail when we are happy with the foundations. You don't build a house by starting with the windows!

be emphasized enough: simplify. There is no situation that cannot be saved by bringing things back down to their simplest elements. By doing this we can discover where we went wrong and just as importantly, how to avoid it happening again.

I know this because it used to bore the pants off me. My impatience was the biggest obstacle to my progress and it took me way too long to recognize this!

A drawing that is well planned and constructed will look right all the way to the last pencil stroke. On the other hand, a drawing with poor foundations will look unconvincing no matter how much extra detail we pile on to it.

We'll look at this concept in a number of ways, at the end of which you should be able to settle on the method which is right for you. This introductory trainer is designed to help you get the most out of the bulk of this book - the creatures themselves.

If you ever find yourself with a drawing that has "run away" from you - when it has all gone horribly wrong - remember the one important rule which can't

This book is broken down into two sections. The first deals exclusively with types of Dragon, the second with other popular mythical creatures. Both sections start with simpler examples and move towards increasingly more complex challenges. All of the creatures follow the same basic approach though: start with the simplest foundations and build methodically towards the fully detailed, finished drawing.

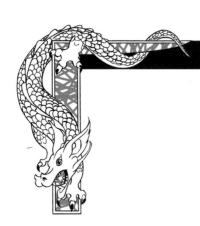

## BASIC BODY PARTS

Whether the creature we want to draw is a type of lizard or a mammal, the most basic components are the same. These comprise a head, neck, torso, tail, forelegs and hind legs.

To the right is a very simplified representation of these body parts as we'd find them in say, a dog. Drawn this simply it's easy to manipulate them into different positions. With no unnecessary details to get in the way, we can easily rotate this basic creature through ninety degrees, from a profile through to a head-on position. If you've never tried this exercise before, it's a great way of improving our understanding of the relationship of objects moving through space.

Try creating your own simple creature and rotating it through space like this. If you're having trouble, remember - simplify! Try doing it first with just the head and torso. When you're happy with those, add the tail. Then add the legs.

This excercise aims to improve our ability to visualize in 3D. If we do enough of this type of exercise and give ourselves new challenges, we'll greatly strengthen this ability and make difficult drawings easy.

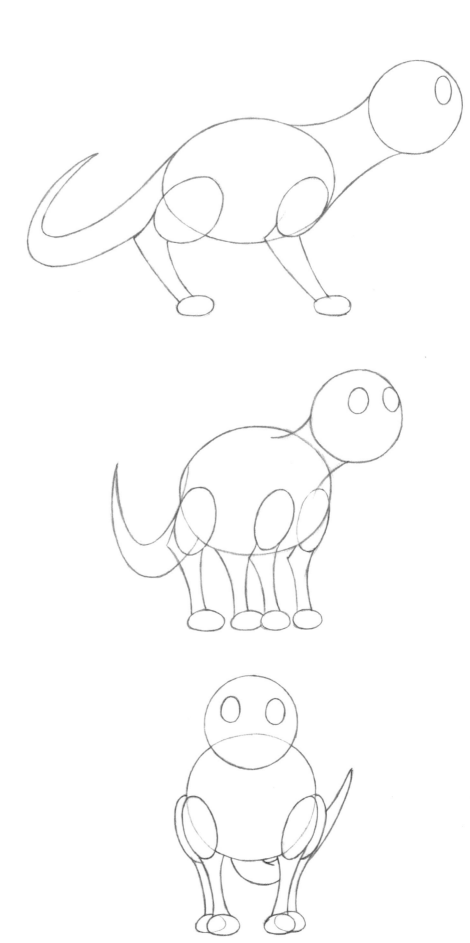

10

If we take the basic "dog" type shape and elongate the main parts we'll have something far more resembling a dragon shape. You could just as easily use this shape for dinosaurs or other lizards. The main difference between these creatures only becomes obvious

a brontosaurus, but dragons are what this book is about, so we've added wings, triangular spines, horns and a segmented underbelly. These are all features you'll find later on as we get to grips with drawing dragons for real.

our final drawing. If you look at the area where the wing joins the shoulder you can see that part of the top of the back will be erased when we finish the drawing. The wing will also "hide" four of the dragon's spines. It's important to draw them though. If we don't, we

when we begin to add the distinguishing features of the particular beast we are drawing.

In the above drawing we've added the distinguishing features of a winged dragon. We could just as easily have used the basic template to create

Another important aspect of these drawings is the fact that they are "drawn through." This means that you can still see the overlapping lines where the various parts join. This is important because if we don't know that these lines definitely join up they'll look wrong in

won't know that the spines are correctly spaced or that the top of the back is correctly aligned. All of these things, if not "drawn through" can contribute to a drawing which just isn't convincing. If the most basic parts don't add up, the finished drawing will suffer.

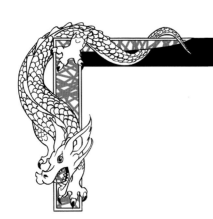

## FLIGHT SCHOOL

Once we've decided on the basic shapes of our creature's body we can then begin to get creative. Keeping everything really simple we can rotate, bend and generally play around with these shapes, putting our creature through the motions.

The only limits to what we can do are dictated by our imagination and the physical limits of what a dragon would be able to do! We can draw from above, from below, from behind or any other angle than occurs to us, knowing that if we follow the basic principles of simplicity our drawings will always look "right."

The drawings on these pages leave out some important earlier stages of creature construction. We'll get to those on the following pages.

For now, just try to see how the same very basic parts have been used to create a number of very different poses. We know we're looking at the same creature in each of them because the component parts are the same. They've just been drawn at radically different angles.

13

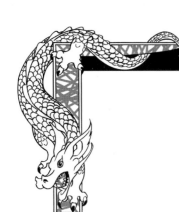

# ground rules

## LINES OF ACTION

The first lines we place on the paper are intentded to establish two things. The first is to establish the general shape and position of the thing we want to draw. The second is to establish the amount of space the drawing will occupy on the paper. There's nothing worse than getting a certain way along in a drawing before realizing we've run out of space.

But the first reason is the really important one. These are called "lines of action" and act as a kind of coathanger, on to which we can "hang" the major body parts. Although these are typically only one or two pencil strokes, they are usually the most important as they dictate everything else that follows.

Once we have a strong visual image in our mind of the thing we want to draw, and the angle we want to draw it at, we lay down a couple of pencil strokes to roughly represent this. These lines, if done right, should say something about the kind of creature we're intending to draw. They are an attempt at a shorthand way of capturing the essense of what we're drawing. When done well, anyone looking should have a reasonable chance of guessing the creature from just these

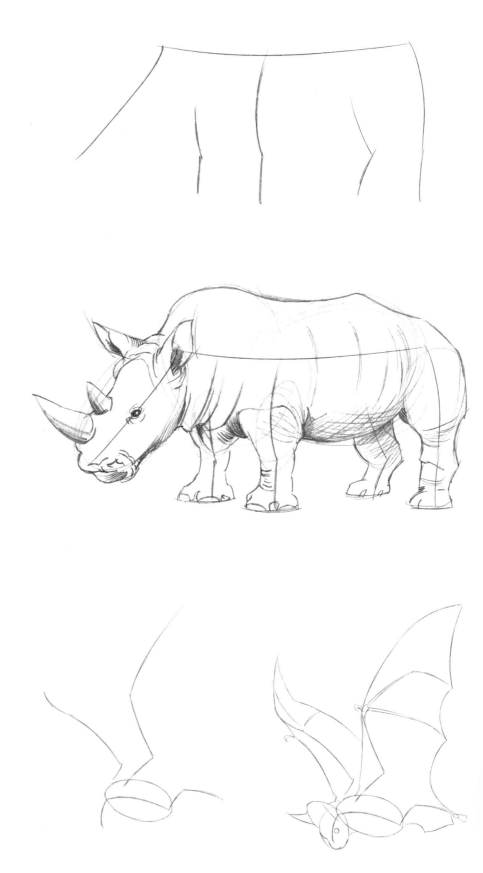

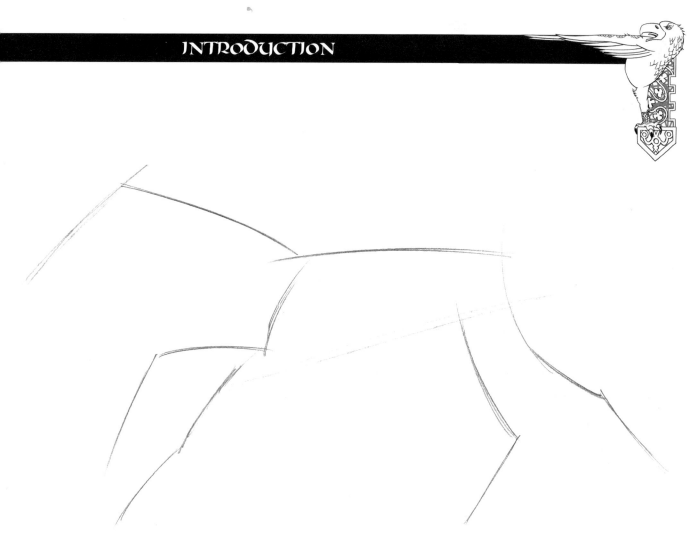

few lines. Can you look at the drawing above and not see a horse?

Not everything we draw is going to be as clear as this, but it gets the point across. Lines of action should ideally be drawn quickly

and with as much expression as possible. Remember - we're going to "hang" the entire drawing on just these few lines!

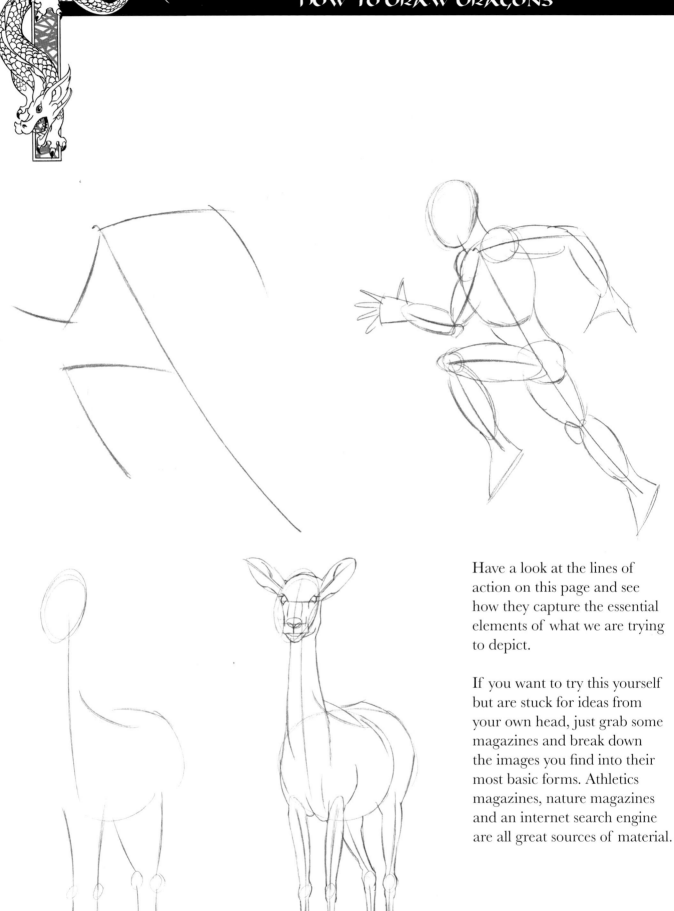

Have a look at the lines of action on this page and see how they capture the essential elements of what we are trying to depict.

If you want to try this yourself but are stuck for ideas from your own head, just grab some magazines and break down the images you find into their most basic forms. Athletics magazines, nature magazines and an internet search engine are all great sources of material.

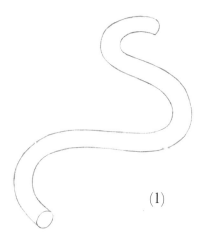

(1)

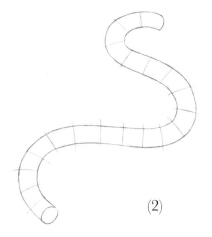

(2)

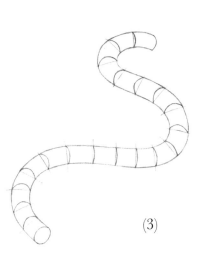

(3)

## SURFACE FORM

In order to "fool" the viewer into believing they are looking at a three-dimensional creature there are several "tricks" we have at our disposal. The most powerful of which is the use of patterns to describe surface form.

An animal's markings will always follow the shape of the creature they cover. Our minds already know this instictively. Experience has taught us to do this without even thinking about it. With a little understanding, we can exploit this to make our drawings more convincing.

The first picture shows a simple worm or snake type creature (1). At the moment it looks quite "flat." There's very little information to guide us as to its shape.

We can do something about this, first by segmenting the snake's body into even sections. The dividing lines all follow the body at right angles to the outline (2).

We can then use these lines as guides to add curves which follow the shape of the snake's body. Notice how the curves are a lot less pronounced when we see them side-on (3).

Next, we draw a line along the length of the body roughly representing the top of the snake. We can then use the lines we now have as guides for the squares which naturally follow the shape of our snake.

Of course, most creatures' markings are not this simplistic, but the principle is the same.

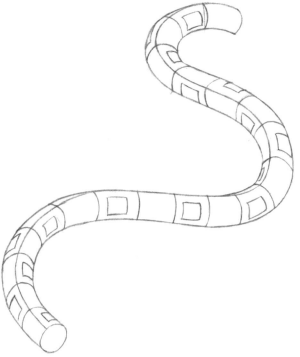

# LIZARD

As a warm-up to the mythical creatures we're going to draw, let's look at a real-life creature and the steps taken from start to finish:

## 1: LINES OF ACTION

These two lines will loosely represent the shape and position of the tail and body.

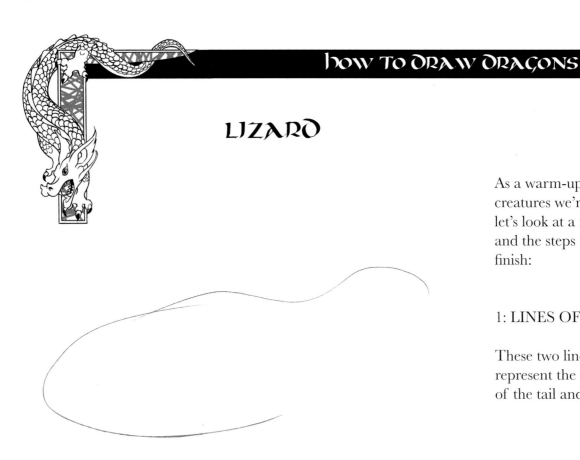

## 2: MAJOR BODY PARTS

As with the rhino on page 14, the torso section is represented by two ovals for the chest/shoulders and rear end respectively. This allows more flexibility than one oval alone would. The lizard's legs are only indicated at this stage.

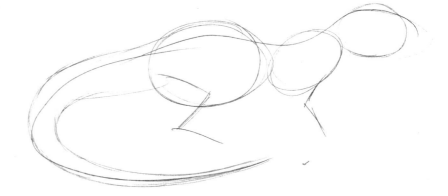

## 3: MINOR BODY PARTS

Here's where we put the flesh on the legs, join the main body parts, indicate the fingers and decide on the shape of the head. We'll indicate where the eye goes too.

## 4: CLEAN-UP

Too many lines can soon become confusing. It's a good idea to tidy things up at some point by carefully erasing the lines we no longer need and firming up the ones we want to keep.

## 5: FIRST DETAILS

Let's finish the fingers and face. We'll segment the tail and "contour map" the lizard's back to help us apply its markings.

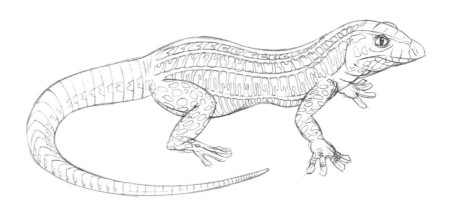

## 6: FINAL DETAILS

Here's where we add all the markings, give some life to the eyes and make any final minor corrections.

All of the creatures in this book follow this same structure with just a few minor differences. The methods we use should allow a degree of adaptability depending on the specific needs and complexity of the subject.

# PART ONE

# DRAGONS

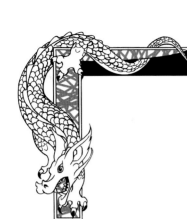

# DRAGON COMPONENTS

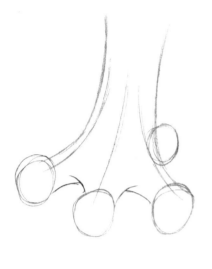

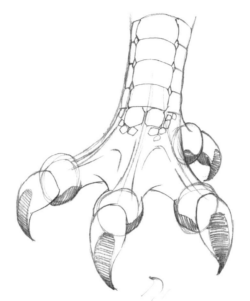

**CLAWS:**
At the wrist the claw splays out and terminates in a ball shape. Out of these come the talons. This is a four-taloned claw, though you can have as many or as few talons as you choose.

**TAIL/SPINE:**
Use the spines to show the twist of the tail. The shape of the spines is very similar to a shark's fin.

**EYE:**
A dragon's eye is much the same as a lizard's. Rather than being a circle like most mammal's, the pupil is much more like a slit.

**WHISKERS:**
How many? The more the merrier as far as I'm concerned. Dragons are supposed to be extravagantly adorned, so go for as many as is practical!

**WINGS:**
A dragon's wings are like an oversized version of a bat's. For real understanding, study these flying mammals to learn how the wings change as they move through the air.

There's an 'elbow' joint from which the vanes of the wing originate. The 'arm' of the wing is usually represented by two 'bones' which curve in opposing directions.

The elbow often terminates in a claw-type protrusion.

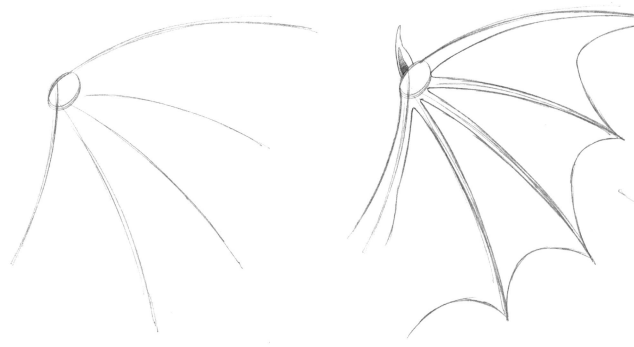

# SIMPLE DRAGON

## 1: LINES OF ACTION

First, we need to establish the lines of action we talked about in the introduction.

The lines to the right represent the most basic position of the wings, body and tail. They only loosely represent the spine and wing bones and simply give us something to "hang" the major body parts on.

## 2: MAJOR BODY PARTS

Now we'll add the basic shapes of the major body parts: wings, body, neck, limbs, head and tail. Start with the head, neck and body, avoiding any detail at this point.

Remember: keep it simple!

24

### 3: MINOR BODY PARTS

This is the point where it starts to look like a dragon!

The snout and jaw is a good place to start. Once you've got these in place it makes it simpler to place the eye correctly. The whiskers or fronds around the head should roughly follow the original circular guidelines, as above.

Next up are the claws. For the moment, just indicate their positions with loose, triangular shapes. We'll work them up more later.

The last thing to take care of at this stage is the shape of the wings. The angles have to be considered here if we're to make them convincing. The right-hand wing looks bigger because we're looking straight at it. The wing on the left though is partly turned away from us, so the curves in the wing shape have been adjusted to show this.

25

## 4: FIRST DETAIL LEVEL

Let's deal with the vanes on
the wings. Notice that the wing
on the left is at a more oblique
angle. This means the curvature
in the vanes will be more
extreme. They should all start
at the "elbow" point halfway up
the wing and end at the points

on the outside of the wing.
Next, let's work on the "mantle"
or spines that run along the
dragon's back and along the
tail. We already have a good idea
of its position from our original
line of action. If your line
doesn't look quite right re-draw
your line running from between
the eyes, along the neck to a

point between the wings and
down into the tail.
The last thing at this stage
is to add the tip of the tail.
Its basically a triangle which
follows the curve line of the tail.

## 5: CLEAN-UP

Now would be a good time to get the eraser out and get rid of all those guidelines we don't need anymore.

You should be able to easily fill in any gaps made by the eraser and have an image similar to the one shown to the left.

Now we're ready to move into phase two.

## 6: SECOND DETAIL LEVEL

Let's get to work on our dragon's head. The details we need to add are: eyes, chin whiskers, nostrils, tongue and lips.

Next, we need to add more definition to the claws and add the two claws halfway up the wings. Finally add the last few small spines to the tail.

## 7: FINAL TOUCHES

The two things left to add are the dragon's scales and its teeth.

The scales should follow the contours of the body, but shouldn't be too uniform. Slight variations in the size of the scales will look more realistic.

You can cover the whole of the dragon's body in scales if you like. I've chosen just to give an impression of them on the head and neck.

Lastly, add some teeth, following the jaw line, with two prominent incisors at the front.

When you're happy you've got everything down, clean up any remaining guidelines and surplus marks with your eraser.

# JAPANESE DRAGON

## 1: LINE OF ACTION

Oriental dragons differ greatly from the classic European varieties. They have long, lean bodies and are usually wingless.

The Japanese dragon type we're going to draw here has a body resembling that of an eel. It's head is far more like a dog's than a lizard's.

Our line of action is essentially an "S" shape with a small, extra hook at the top.

Try and draw this line as quickly and spontaneously as possible.

## 2: MAJOR BODY PARTS

Using the "S" shape as your guide, draw the outline of the body. Just do this roughly, as much of the body's outline will become obscured later when we draw the dragon's "mane."

Using an oval and a roughly oblong shape, indicate the position of the head.

Lastly, show the position and shape of the limbs. One of the hind legs will be obscured completely by the body, so we only need to draw three limbs.

Next, let's add the main features of the head and face: a nose, the bottom jaw, two horns and ears.

## 4: FIRST DETAIL LEVEL
(opposite page, above)

Before finishing the limbs we need to add the long, distinctive whiskers. As you draw them you should imagine them twisting and being blown backwards by the force of the wind. It's really important to make sure you get them to taper evenly as you move from the face to their tips.

Once we've got the whiskers down we can then finish off the limbs, dealing with the basic details of shoulders, claws etc. Add a claw-like appendage at the elbow. Use the curve of the claws to indicate their direction.

We need to add some fur at the point where the head meets the body. This should run from the ear down to the jaw line and like the mane should point backwards with the wind direction.

Our dragon will have a "ribbed" underside, so let's add some lines indicating where the upper body meets the underside.

Finally, indicate the position of the bottom lip. This will also act as the guideline for the dragon's teeth.

## 3: INTERMEDIATE LEVEL

We need to add the dragon's mane before we go any further. This should be a loosely bunched strip of fur running from the back of the head right down to the tip of the tail. As we want to give the impression of the dragon moving through the air, the tips of the fur should all be pointing backwards.

Now let's add some meat to the bones of the two most prominent limbs. Don't get too detailed at this moment though, as we need to add one more feature that will partly cover the limbs.

Tip: your hands will inevitably pick up some graphite from the artwork while you're working. Before you clean up your drawings, wash your hands. That way, you won't "spread the lead" and you'll end up with a much cleaner drawing.

## 5: CLEAN-UP

We've got lots of guidelines we no longer need, so let's get busy with the eraser before adding the final details.

Now the mane is nice and tidy we'll add that other forelimb. While we're at it, let's make the upper lip, chin and top of the head slightly furry.

## 6: FINAL DETAILS

To finish up, we need some more furry detail on the face, as well as more fur detail on our dragon's mane.

We also need to segment the creature's underbelly. The curves on these segments need to follow the shape of the body. For tips on this refer back to page 17.

Next, we need to finish off the detail on those claws. These are in the form of scales and like the underbelly should wrap around the wrists and claws, following their shape.

Finally, our Japanese dragon needs some teeth. We've already drawn the shape of the lips so we can use this line as a guide for the teeth. Make sure you get some big canines in there! One more simple line can be used for the tongue.

# BABY DRAGON

This is a different kind of challenge. Even dangerous fire-breathing lizards can be cute when they're kids, but we need to bring out these characteristics.

## 1: LINES OF ACTION

A seriously curly line would be appropriate for a baby dragon, so let's start with that. It would add some cuteness to make baby's tummy stick out too, so we'll work that into our line.

## 2: MAJOR BODY PARTS

This is the stage where we work on getting the proportions right. A big head and small body says "cute baby" so that's exactly what we'll have. A stubby, curvaceous snout will work too. We'll give him a slightly grumpy, downturned mouth while we're at it.

The wings and tail should be as curvy as possible as well.

## 3: MINOR BODY PARTS—1

Let's begin with our baby
dragon's limbs. His arms should

The wings are standard dragon
issue, albeit in a more compact
form. Let's have the usual horn
at the wing's elbow as well.

than on an adult. We'll put a
small indent at the lower front
of the beak/snout. We also
need to put in the lower jaw
which should have the same
curvature as the bottom of the
upper jaw.

be small and not very powerful.
His hind legs should be much
bulkier, especially around the
buttocks. As his tummy is
protruding it will make visual
sense if his legs are pointing
backwards. Let's make his toes
curl backwards too.

We'll indicate the vanes which
flow from the "elbow" to the
wing tips.

We should start the face by
placing the eye correctly.
It should be a little bigger
relatively to the dragon's head

The ears will be like miniature
versions of the wings in their
construction, but for now we'll
just put them in as a basic shape.

## 4: MINOR BODY PARTS - 2

The one obvious addition to our picture at this stage are the spines running from the top of baby's head down to the tip of the tail  About a third of the

at their smallest at their start and end points.

The line running from the back of the jaw to about halfway down the tail represents the perimeter of the underbelly.

Lastly on the face we need to add a tongue, a lizard-like shape forming the eye opening and a narrow slit-like pupil at the center of the eye.

We then need to firm up the

way down the tail the spines begin to veer off as the tail is free to curl and wind. They reappear  around the other side about another quarter of the way down. They are at their largest on the dragon's back and

For the ears, we'll add a couple of vanes at the center and then scoop out the edges to form the ears points. The ear on the other side is hardly showing so requires no modification.

hands and feet and indicate some claws.

Lastly, finish up the vanes of the wings and tighten up the tail.

## 5: CLEAN UP

It's time to carefully erase all those guidelines we no longer need. Tighten up what remains with a sharp pencil.

## 6: FINAL DETAILS - 1

We'll concentrate on the final facial details at this stage.

As the tongue is inside the mouth we'll make that darker. Let's do the same to the hook of our baby's beak too.

Our dragon still lacks a proper nose so we need to add a small, baby nostril. To accommodate this, we'll modify the top of the snout, increasing the size of the "bump."

Let's strengthen the vanes on the ears and add a quizzical eyebrow. Let's also double up the line surrounding the eye to give it some extra dimension.

If we add two little white circles to the pupils before filling in with black this will provide a glint to the eye.

The last thing we'll do at this stage is put in the segments of the underbelly.

## 7: FINAL DETAILS - 2

Finally, we need to give our baby a fine coat of lizard skin. This is achieved by using lines in two directions, both of which follow the contours of the dragon's body.

We should try to draw all of the lines in one direction first before starting to draw those in the other direction. This is because it's really hard to make sense of things if we're not certain that the lines in at least one direction are correct.

Notice where the body parts bulge out, such as the thigh, the space between the lines increases. This concept is based on the same principles as those shown on page 17. Conversely, the lines get finer and closer together as they move towards the tip of the tail.

When using this technique it's a good idea to avoid having the lines cross at right angles. This tends to look like the work of an amateur.

To finish up, add some shadowing under the vanes of the wing and on the foot farthest away.

The last thing to do is add some varied tone to the spine and you're done.

# SLEEPING DRAGON

One of the mainstays of fantasy novels and films is the sleeping dragon that the hero has to avoid awakening at all costs.

But a sleeping dragon is more than just a dragon lying down. The sleep position has unique characteristics. Animals tend to sleep on their paws with as much of their bodies tucked in as possible. This is usually to preserve body heat, so whether a creature that can breathe fire needs to do this is debatable. Nonetheless, as with the rest of the creatures in this book, we are drawing on aspects of the natural world in order to communicate ideas already understood by everyone about behavior.

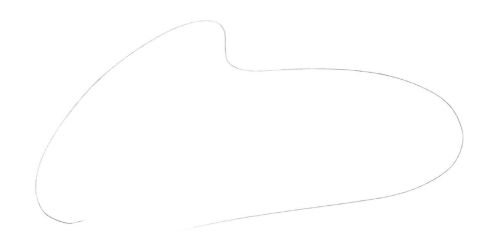

## 1: LINE OF ACTION

We know our sleeping dragon is going to form a loose circle. As the dragon's back is going to be the highest point we need to establish where this is going to occur. As always, try to draw this single line quickly.

## 2: MAJOR BODY PARTS - 1

The largest circular shape represents the biggest area of the dragon's body when in this sleeping position. It's the point where the back meets the hind quarters.

The second largest circle represents the position and size of the head. A loose, slightly

curved shape indicates the dragon's snout.

There are two smaller circles under the head which will later become the front paws.

The one visible arm is only loosely indicated by a couple of lines for now. A couple of loose lines roughly indicate the position and shape of the thigh.

An "S" shaped line runs in front of the head and nearest paw showing the position of the tail.

The shape of the back is greatly consolidated. There is a very steep dip in the back as it moves from the hind quarters towards the shoulders. We'll indicate the point where the center of the curving neck joins the head.

Next, we'll put some meat on that forearm and join the shoulder to the body.

At the other end, we'll get some more substance into that tail, especially where it tucks under the chin and moves out

directly under the head and put in the position of the dragon's fingers.

Now, on to the head. First is the placing of the eye. Once we've done this we can add a couple of lines showing where the ears will appear.. We can also add the mouth, remembering that the lower jaw is much shallower than the upper part. The last part of the face to work on is the creation of the bump which forms the nose.

## 3: MAJOR BODY PARTS - 2

This stage is mainly a firming up of what already exists plus the addition of some smaller anatomical parts.

towards the viewer. Let's also more firmly establish the shape of that big hind leg and tuck it behind the tail.

For now, we'll just loosely show some knuckles on the paw

By now, your dragon should be looking quite relaxed. If there's a stiffness to it, if it doesn't look totally comfortable, try to figure out why by looking at the creature's overall balance.

## 4: MINOR BODY PARTS - 1

If we're happy with the overall pose using the basic body parts it's time to get into the smaller details.

antenna behind the dragon's head and ear.

Next, we'll draw the basic shape of the most visible ear. We'll leave the other ear alone until after we've done the spines. While we're in the area, let's

so let's work in some nostrils to fit in this space. We'll also emphasize this shape by adding a wrinkle between the bump and the first horn.

We'll make a start on the claws that protrude from the paw under the chin.

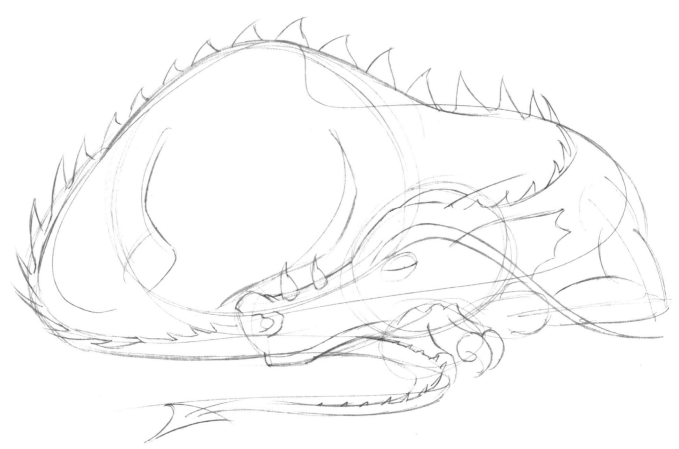

Let's continue on with the head. The antennae that look like giant, overgrown eyebrows should be made to droop and lay on the ground. This can only add to the relaxed look of our dragon. They need to flow out of the shape of the head and taper evenly as they move towards the ground. We can make out part of the other

put in a simple, curved line indicating the closed eye.

At the other end of the head we want to add a couple of decorative horns. These should be a similar shape to canine teeth - tapering, but with a bulge at the base.

We've already put in a bump to indicate the tip of the nose,

Lastly, we'll get to work on the spines running from the neck to the tail. We should try to vary the angle of these as they weave their way down the animal's back. At the point where the chin rests on the tail we can use the spines to show the tail has been pulled inward.

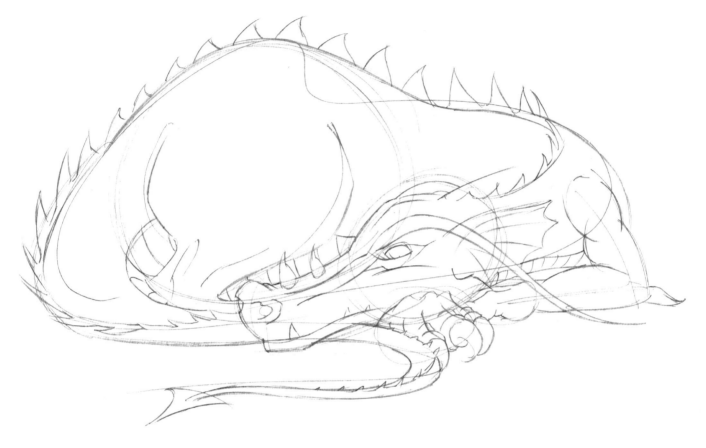

## 5: MINOR BODY PARTS - 2

Let's first establish the separation line between the upper body and the underbelly. There are three areas where the underbelly is exposed so we need to work out the curvature for these parts.

Next, we'll add some bone and tendon detail to the bottom of the hind leg. We'll also finish the formation of the partly hidden front paw and add some knuckle and claw detail to the foremost paw. Let's add a decorative elbow spike at the far right of the picture.

That just leaves finishing off the head. We need to add quite

a bit of detail to the eye area. First, let's surround the eye with a decorative shape and then add a couple of ridges running along the snout. The paw that the head is resting on is having the effect of pushing up the flesh of the dragon's cheek, so we'll add

a line under the eye that makes this more noticeable.

Lastly, we need to add some teeth. A big canine near the front and two smaller teeth further back.

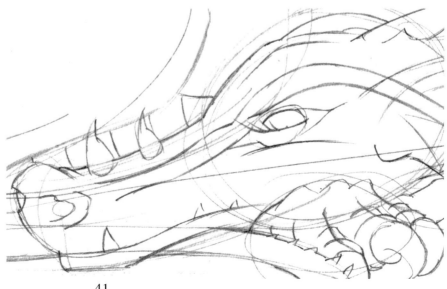

41

# SLEEPING DRAGON

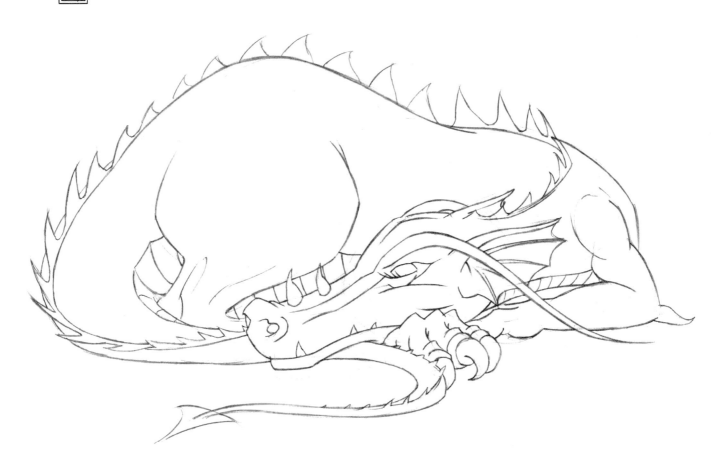

## 6: CLEAN UP

That's about as long as is practical to leave it before getting the eraser out for a much needed clean up. We need to finish off that far ear and generally tighten up before we can move on to the patterning. We should aim to get our picture as clean as possible at this point as the pattern we're going to create will make it doubly hard to make corrections afterwards.

## 7: FINAL DETAILS

The final detail for this creature involves covering our dragon with a multitude of circular shapes. Although these shapes don't look much by themselves we can employ them to help us very effectively describe all the varying contours of our sleeping beast's body shape.

Take a look at the close-up image to the right. See how it seems to bulge outwards at the center? This is achieved using a combination of size and shape.

The best way to really understand how and why this works is to draw similar sized circles on a deflated balloon.

Blow the balloon up and then look at it with one eye closed. You'll see the same effect. The closer to the edge of the balloon, the more the shapes will "flatten out" due to the changing angle you are viewing them from.

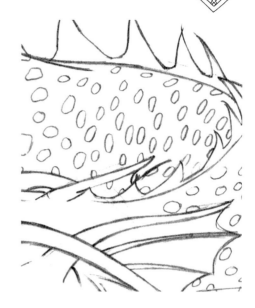

The close-up image on the right is another detail of the finished dragon, this time showing the neck/shoulder area. As the neck curves round towards us the shapes become narrower, helping to establish the three dimensionality of the dragon's body.

Needless to say, you don't have to use these shapes. You can use just about anything that lends itself to "useful distortions." You could cover your dragon with buttercups or smiley faces if you wish, but this would probably distract a little too much from the drawing.

To practice this technique at your leisure, why not scan or photocopy the unadorned image opposite? You can then experiment to your heart's content until you achieve perfection.

If the pose itself is still giving you a hard time it's worth studying sleeping animals. If you don't have a cat or dog at home then study a friend's pet or search online for other suitable images.

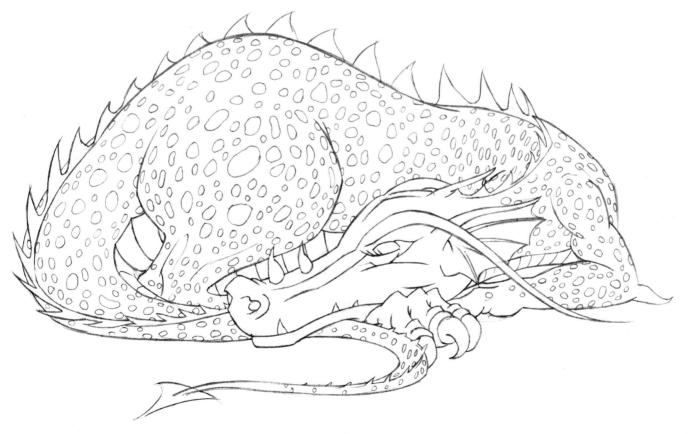

# chinese dragon

Chinese dragons are completely unlike Western dragons. Where the Western variety are angry, the Chinese ones are wild. Where Western dragons are purposeful, Chinese dragons are untameable free spirits.

Like the Japanese dragons they are rarely winged, but gain the power of flight by simply being spiritual creatures rather than the very physical lizard-like dragons of the West. They can fly simply because gravity is meaningless to them! They tend to "swim" through the air rather than fly through it.

When the Chinese depict dragons as part of a design, their attitude to anatomy is far less grounded in conventional biology than the average Western approach. It is the overall shape and impact of the dragon that is the important thing. This is important to keep in mind when drawing dragons like the one depicted on the following pages.

## 1: LINE OF ACTION

This has to be the craziest line of action in this book! This dragon has an extremely flexible spine, so we can really take some liberties with it.

Notice that our line roughly occupies a square.

## 2: MAJOR BODY PARTS
(previous page, below)

Indicate the position and size of the head with a small oval as shown. This oval should be at a similar angle to the line we've created.

Using the original line of action as a guide, outline the body. Notice the body is thinner at the neck and is at its thickest about one-third of the way down. From this point it should gently taper towards the tip of the tail.

Now for those crazy limbs. Make sure your guidelines show them splayed out in wild abandon!

## 3: MINOR BODY PARTS - 1

Starting with the head, we need to work out where the snout and lower jaw line are positioned. See how the snout follows the direction of the original line of action? While we're here, we may as well roughly indicate the whiskers which fly forward wildly from the nose.

Our dragon is going to have a thick mantle of feather-like decorations flowing from the back of its head. Just put these in loosely for now.

We now need to get some flesh on those limbs. Although they are all pointing in different directions, we needn't get too hung up on their anatomical correctness. Just concentrate

on their shape for the moment. Three out of four of the dragon's paws are going to be splayed like five-pointed stars, so let's make a start on those. The other paw is going to be a side view with the back claw sticking out in the opposing direction.

The tail also has a claw-like termination, so lightly pencil that in.

## 4: MINOR BODY PARTS - 2

We can't have a blind dragon, so without further ado let's get some eyes into that head. Notice the upturned crescents at the corners of the eyes.

Next on the list is getting some more shape into our dragon's snout. Two gentle curves form two sections. Let's flesh out those whiskers too.

At either side of the dragon's head put in some fur curling towards the direction of its

"wobbly" quality to them almost like an oak leaf. The fourth, side view foot at bottom right is equally wobbly even though the toes are together.

You may have noticed a new curved line running down the body a little above halfway.

Next, we'll do some work on the lower jaw. Put in four or five ridges in along the bottom of the jaw line and two curves on the facing side.

mantle. Lastly on the head, add a big, curly tongue.

Now we'll get some shape to those fingers. These look almost nothing like other dragon claws in this book. They have a

This represents the part of the spine that becomes visible as the dragon's body turns. We'll add the adornments in a couple of stages time.

## 5: MINOR DETAILS - 1

This is the point where we get into all the teeth, claws and other small stuff.

At the end of the nose is a bizarre kind of moustache, made up of a group of curly

How do we know which of our dragon's claws is the thumb? It's the only one with the talon facing in the opposite direction (2). All of the talons follow a loosely circular pattern.

You may also have noticed the shaggy fur I've added to the

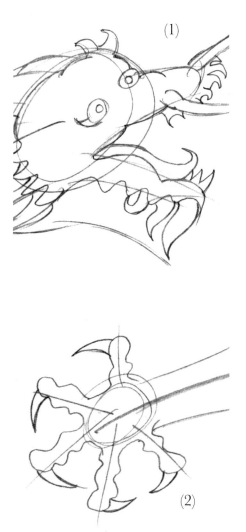

fronds (1). Seldom found on Western type dragons, these are typical of Chinese ones. We have three big, fat whiskers coming out from under the chin and three visible teeth, too.

upper arms and upper legs (3). This should start small and get bigger as it moves towards the elbows and knees.

## 6: CLEAN UP

There's a lot of messy lines on our drawing now, so get that eraser out and clean it up. Touch up any weak spots with a freshly sharpened pencil.

## 7: MINOR DETAILS - 2

Let's finish off the mantle. You'll notice two "horns" which now come out of the back of the head. As with most things on

a Chinese dragon they bear little resemblance to the kind of horns you'd find on a Western dragon. The extra segments on them help separate them from the rest of the mantle.

Our dragon's lips need addressing. These should be a little fatter at the point where they join (1), tapering towards the chin/nose.

Next, we're going to add some fire to those eyes. Directly above are the flame like eyelashes. Coming out of the corner of

the nearest eye is a decorative squiggle which serves to draw attention to the eyes (2).

The two paws on the left-hand side are facing palms out and have had a couple of curved lines added to indicate this.

Lastly, we need to add the small, bony appendages to the spine. Every fourth appendage is a tooth-shaped spine, the rest are simple ovals. Although these run from the neck to the tail they are only visible when the body turns as previously mentioned on page 46.

HORNS

PALMS OUT

2

1

## 8: FINAL DETAILS

All that's left to do is add the contoured "scales" that cover our dragon's body. Much the same technique that was described on page 37 is used to achieve this. As before, you should try to draw all the lines in one direction before drawing those in the opposite direction to avoid bewilderment.

The process usually takes some thinking through, as we try to see in our minds where the various changes in the contours of the twisting body occur.

Done correctly, this technique should tell the viewer everything they need to know about the direction and shape of your drawing.

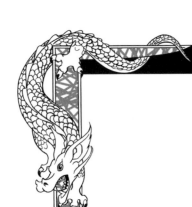

# dragon head

Now for something a little different. We're going to concentrate on one particular body part. It's the big, fat head of a Western dragon and great practice for anyone who really wants to get into the details.

It's probably not the toughest thing to draw in this book, but it's still quite complex, so we'll take it slowly.

## 1: LINES OF ACTION

These simple shapes lay out all the major parts and provide the "coat hanger" for the main body parts. As with all the lines of action, try to draw them quickly and without fuss.

## 2: MAJOR BODY PARTS

As we're drawing a close-up of a head, it's a good idea to get the placement of the eye positioned early on.

We'll use the bottom of our rough circle as a guide for the back of our dragon's jaw. With a simple curve in the opposite direction we'll put in the bottom of the jaw line and join this to the original guide with another small curve.

Next up is the nose, or beak part of the head. As with the bottom jaw, we'll use a curved

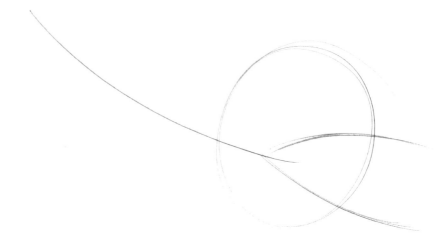

line running from our original rough circle towards the nose and then finish this off with two downward curving lines for the "beak."

Now to the neck. Although the neck gets narrower as it moves

from the body to the neck, just as it joins the head there is a slight widening. Use the original line of action as your kind and keep this in mind.

There's a curved line running from the back of the jaw up

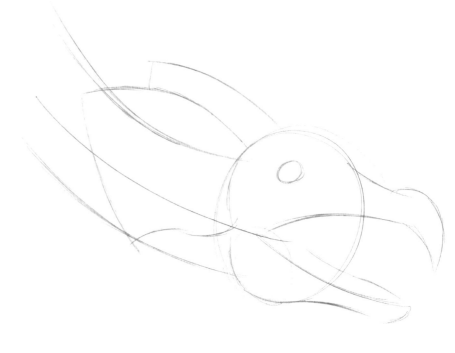

to the original circle. This line completes the basic head.

The nearest ear is attached at the meeting points of the lines at the back of the head and just above the neckline behind the eye.

The antenna at the back is mostly hidden by the head and the ear.

Draw in the three vanes inside the ear and then use these as guides to scoop out the sections that form the points of the ear.

If we continue this line between the ears we can add a few, smaller shark fin spines on top of the head.

The last thing at this stage is to get just a little more shape into the dragon's nose. The curved

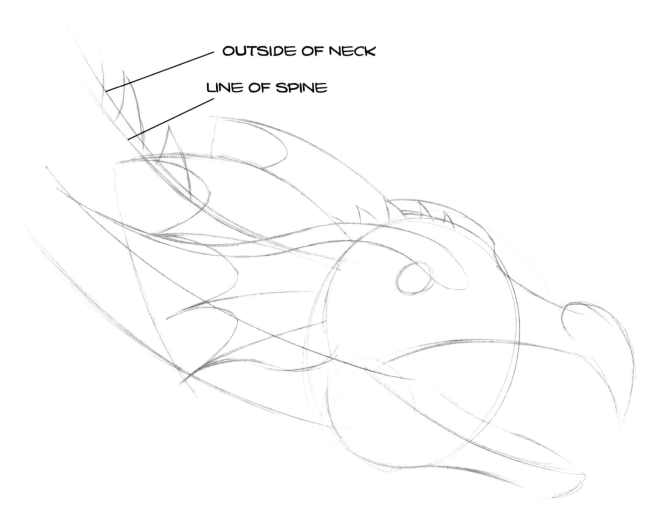

OUTSIDE OF NECK

LINE OF SPINE

### 3: MINOR BODY PARTS - 1

Start with the two antennae. These function like eyebrows and should have the same expressive quality. They should curve one way and then the other and be drawn as fluidly as possible.

No vanes are needed for the other ear, just one scoop for the part that shows.

There are two lines making up the top of the neck. The one below represents the center line where the spines run towards the body. Put in these shark fin shaped spines along this line.

line we're adding here will dictate the shape of the nostrils.

## 4: MINOR BODY PARTS - 2

It's time for the teeth. To give them shape and character, these kind of teeth are in two

their prey. Save the two biggest pairs for the front of the top and bottom jaws respectively.

The two horns on our dragon's nose are of a very similar shape, albeit fatter and larger.

backwards, but as our previous Chinese model showed, on crazier dragons they can go in any direction. I've put three whiskers on the jowls and one either side of the chin, but feel free to experiment with either more or less.

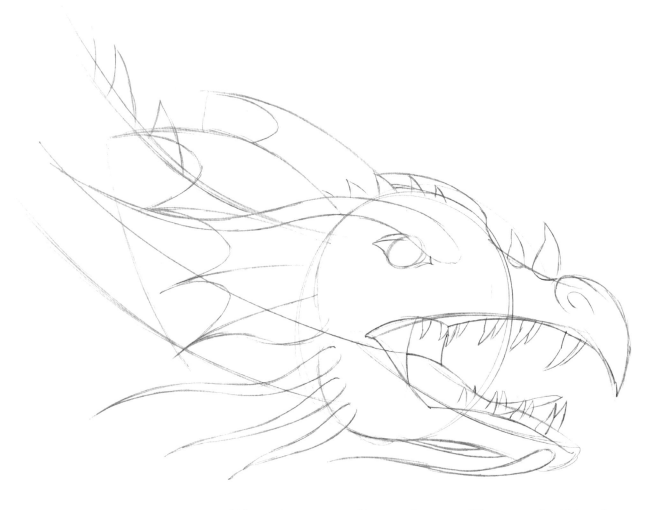

sections. The bottom half has a slight bulge to them. The top half is a more straightforward shark fin shape. This has the effect of giving them dimension while at the same time making them nice and sharp. The teeth of a carnivore generally face backwards to help them hold

We need to start working on the eye at this point too. Add a flap of skin above the eye as well as the decorative shape that the eye sits in.

Now for some whiskers. These are of a similar shape to the antennae. They usually face

The curve signifying the position of the nostril mirrors the larger one we drew in the previous stage.

There is a flap of flesh which fits into the corners of the mouth. When you've put these in, finish by putting in the tongue.

5: CLEAN UP!

6: FINAL DETAIL - 1

Finish off the vanes of the ears. Add some gums for the teeth to sit in and put in the separating line on the throat. We need some lips too.

Add the pupil to the eye and more detail to the area surrounding the eyeball.

The rest of this stage is concerned with mapping out the areas where we are going to apply different types of scales. As a rule the softer parts of the face will have smaller, spongier scales. The harder parts will have larger, squarer scales.

## 7: FINAL DETAILS - 2

Work on the bigger, rougher scales first. Although they too forced. Try using some very light guidelines to help you if you're having trouble planning the shape and direction of your scales.

## 8: FINAL DETAILS - 3

Now we'll deal with the squashier, softer parts of the face, of which the eye is the most obvious example.

should follow the contours of the respective parts of the face, this should not be done too clinically. In order to get a naturalistic effect we should think of the contouring of the scales as a *tendency* rather than an absolute rule. This way we get the effect of showing the shape, but without it looking

As the scales move upward from the bridge of the nose towards the fleshier part of the top of the head, the scales become looser and lumpier.

To get the effect of the scaly lips we have to imagine the dividing lines curling towards the inside of the mouth.

The scales around the eye radiate out getting larger as they do so. If you're having trouble doing this freehand, draw some light guidelines indicating these rings. Notice that although the area surrounding the eye is wider in some places than others, the number of scales doesn't change.

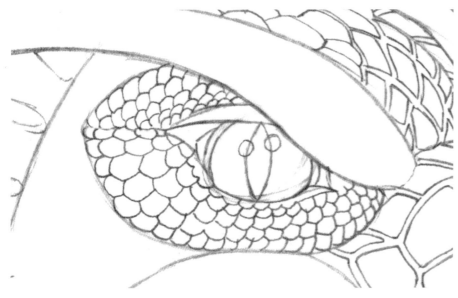

invaluable insight into how these tricky anatomical details actually work.

The other, softer parts of the face are not quite so organized as the area around the eye but they still follow the principle discussed back on page 42.

This means that the wider areas naturally have wider scales.

To really get an understanding of these principles take a look at nature. Studying the heads of real reptiles gives us an

## 9: FINAL DETAILS - 4

The only thing left to do now is to add some scales to our dragon's neck. If you've worked

neck. Another thing to watch out for is to keep the spacing even. A sudden change in gap width will have an unwanted, jarring effect.

Phew. That was a lot of work. By now you should have an

For our last dragon we have a real challenge. Something that pulls all of these techniques together. It will test not only your understanding of all the principles we've looked at so far but also your ability to organize your work and maintain control

your way through this book you should by now be familiar with the technique used to achieve this.

The angle of the curves need to follow the gentle bend in the

impressive arsenal of techniques for creating dragons. You should be able to not only build a dragon from scratch but also be able to give it a thoroughly convincing hide, whether scaly, spotty or otherwise.

over it. This ability to avoid a complex piece of art running away from us is one of the final hurdles to our becoming fully-fledged artists.

# FIRE BREATHING DRAGON

This one's a classic. We're going to draw a full-blown scaly, winged, mean-spirited Western-type dragon breathing a big fireball directly at us.

This is the toughest dragon in the book and requires good planning and a constantly sharp pencil. We're going to be cramming a lot of detail in so we'll be working a little larger than usual.

## 1: LINES OF ACTION

First, we need to get a very clear idea in our minds of what we want our dragon to look like. It might be a good idea to quickly doodle some possible poses to make sure we have the pose fixed in our minds before laying down our initial lines of action.

The central "U" shape represents the position of the body, with the loops either side forming the neck and tail.

As our dragon is going to be looking straight at us, the oval shape representing it's head should be upright and the neckline where it attaches needs to straight also.

## 2: MAJOR BODY PARTS - 1

Start by establishing the position of the torso, the top of which is about halfway up the head. The chest and tummy are made up essentially of two separate ovals

similar to the two used on page 18. Once the torso is in place it's a fairly simple case of following our guideline to put the flesh on the neck.

The most visible hind leg follows the curve of the body, starting from behind the tummy.

The tail should also be a simple case of following our original guideline, flowing out of the torso from behind the hind leg. Continue the belly line through the leg to form the other side of the tail.

The shoulders, arms, hands and feet are, for the moment, indicated only as simple shapes. Their position is the only important thing to consider at this stage.

The leg which is mostly hidden behind the body should ideally form part of an imaginary line between the tummy and the knee of the other leg. This will give it the appearance of being tucked in and tidy.

## 3: MAJOR BODY PARTS—2

These wings are a little more complex than previous ones as they're partially folded, showing both the inside and outside of

Because the body is tilted at an angle, the outer section will be larger on the right-hand wing than the left. Once we establish these two lines it's a simple case of putting in the

We can begin to start working up the hands and feet at this point too using simple shapes to work out the positions of the fingers and toes. I've made this a four-toed/fingered dragon,

the wing. The best place to start is at the shoulders, to form the major bones up to the "elbow" joint. From there, we can draw the outsides of the wing giving us the bulk of the wing's shape.

undersides of the wings. Use guidelines to establish the shape of the wings as per previous dragons if you're unconfident about putting these lines straight down. See page 26.

but feel at liberty to use either less or more as you wish.

Add two light guidelines for the facial features and put in the nose and jaw as shown.

## 4: CLEAN UP

We've created enough overlapping lines now to justify getting busy with the eraser.

## 5: MINOR BODY PARTS - 1

We're going to work on the rest of the major facial features now.

If we start by putting the eyes in first, these and the nose will provide good points of reference for the rest of the features.

The antennae on top of our dragon's head double as both eyebrows and horns.

There are two pairs of serious whiskers coming out of the back of the jaw and a smaller pair emanating from the chin.

We need to put in two curved lines joining the upper jaw to the lower jaw.

The nose starts wide at the bridge, tapering sharply due to the effect of foreshortening. A couple of simple lines will be enough for the nostrils for the moment.

The ears join the head just behind the eyes and out of sight

behind the antennae. The curve in them changes direction about halfway up.

Lastly, add the talons. For some help with these, check page 22.

On the ears, first draw the part which joins to the head and runs to the tips. Then put the other vanes in, finally scooping out the small sections between them.

It's about time we finished the vanes on those wings now that most of the minor body parts are established.

## 6: MINOR BODY PARTS—2

Let's get some life into those eyes in the form of some pupils.

We'll also divide the nose into two sections and give the nostrils some more body.

Draw a line from the center of the back of the head running up the neck. This should disappear over the "horizon" as the neck twists round. Use this line to place the spines. Add a couple more small horns at the top of the head.

Finally, draw the segments of the underbelly reflecting all the changes in direction.

## 7: FINAL DETAILS - 1

I told you our dragon would be spitting out a blazing fireball. Well, now's the time to start putting it in place.

First draw the rough circle at the foot of the drawing. We need to draw a straight, tapering line from the inside of the dragon's mouth to the circle. This line should suddenly taper much more severely as it gets near the circle.

Next we need to prevent our dragon from remaining toothless. Put a big pair of canines at the front of the bottom jaw. The teeth should generally curve inwards.

The scales on the neck and body are particularly complex on this dragon, so I've decided to show the lines in one direction first. Ideally they should line up either side of the spine in order to create a consistent pattern. The lines are at a consistent thirty degrees approximately and run down as far as the shoulder. At this point the type of scale changes to the ones that cover the body.

As with previous scale patterns we should be absolutely happy with those running in one direction before adding those running in the other. It can be an absolute nightmare trying to make sense of so many lines so close together if things go wrong.

We can add some tendons to both the feet and hands as well.

Tendons run from a central point at the wrist or ankle towards the fingers or toes that they serve.

## 8: FINAL DETAILS - 2

To give some body to our fireball we need to add some small, wavy lines that follow the shape of the ball. Less at the center and more at the edges will give some real shape to the fireball. Add a few small plumes coming off the side and we've got a great ball of fire.

The scales covering the body initially use the same technique as for the neck. Where they differ is that they have been made to overlap with the scale beneath it. This way they look more like a kind of organic armor plating.

# PART TWO

# OTHER CREATURES

# GIANT OCTOPUS

Of all the mythical creatures in this book the one most likely to actually exist is the Giant Octopus. Huge specimens have been found washed up on beaches or dredged up in fishermen's nets.

Whether such creatures could grow to the kind of size necessary to drag large ocean-going vessels to a watery doom is debatable. Yet not all such mariner's yarns are easily dispelled.

The largest giant octopus actually measured was 9.6 meters arm-to-arm, or around 31 feet. Pretty big, but nothing on one specimen washed up on a beach in the Bahamas which, judged only from surviving photographic records, was estimated to be at least 150 feet long!

Drawing a creature like this presents us with an entirely different kind of challenge to that of a dragon. With eight tentacles to contend with, all of which overlap each other, the potential for visual confusion is greatly increased.

## 1: LINES OF ACTION

The first thing to get established is the octopus' mantle, represented by the large oval at the right of the image. Although

we naturally think of this part as the creature's head, it is in fact more like its body, containing as it does the octopus' internal organs. It needs to be angled at the same degree that we want the tentacles to flow from.

As we want our octopus to be active, the tentacles need to flow outward from the body in a fairly chaotic way. Some will be more foreshortened, others less so, making for an apparent variety in length.

All of the tentacles though are variations on the "S" shape. Giving them a more extreme curve near the tips of

the tentacles has the effect of making them look probing and expressive.

## 2: MAJOR BODY PARTS

The first thing we need to do is work out which tentacles are in front of others, using outlines to separate them. Where the tentacles join the body we have to be careful to keep these angles "soft": there should be no hard lines on our octopus.

Once we're happy with the tentacles we should loosely indicate the position of the eyes. These appear as bulges at the front of the mantle.

Underneath the mantle and eyes is another part of our creature. This part contains the gill slit where the octopus takes in water. This will become clear in the next stages.

## 3: CLEAN UP

It's unusual to clean up so early in a drawing, but with those loose tentacles flying around and lots of detail to add to them we need to make life as easy for ourselves as we can.

Remember to firm up any weak points after erasing with a sharp pencil.

## 4: MINOR BODY PARTS—1

The first thing we'll do at this point is more firmly establish

the eyes. Form a bridge between them with two small, curved lines as shown. Then place the eyeball at the center of the right-hand bulge.

Below this eye is the aforementioned gill slit. This is a quite complex valve-like structure. For now, just indicate it with a couple of well placed curves.

Next, we need to give some more shape to the actual body of the octopus. The lines running from below the eyes down the shafts of the tentacles not only add some dimension, they also add tension to the

tentacles, giving an indication of physical effort being exerted. They'll also be used as guides for the final details later on.

The tentacles are in need of some suckers. The tiny ones towards the tips will take care of themselves, but the larger ones need a little planning.

First we need to establish some lines representing the division between the top and the underside of the tentacles. Only four out of eight tentacles are sufficiently raised to show off their suckers. The remaining ones are either on the sea floor or the suckers are facing away from us.

The small, transverse lines represent the spacing of the major suckers. Obviously, the space between them should diminish as the tentacles move towards their tips.

## 5: MINOR BODY PARTS—2

All we're going to do at this stage is add all the suckers. At this point they're just crude ovals; we'll add more detail later.

If you look at a photograph of an octopus' tentacles you'll notice that they are not an even, predictable size. We shouldn't therefore try to make them too perfect or even as this will result in an overly formal, almost forced result.

Notice that the ovals become narrower the more they face away from us. Head on they're almost circles.

## 6: ADDED EXTRAS

There's no doubt that by now what we've got is an octopus. But what makes it a *giant octopus*?

disembodied and fail to interact with our creature. Just draw straight over the tentacles as the blown-up detail shows. We'll clean it up before moving into the final details stage.

The other thing we're going to get more detail into at this stage is the eye/gill slit area. We've added an eyelid and some creases/bags under the creature's eye. We've also added

several folds of skin around the gill slit. This has the effect of making it look like a weird kind of mouth; another distinctively cephalopod feature.

What we need is something to give an idea of *scale*. Enter two fearless divers, complete with wet-suits and aqualungs. These are constructed the same way as everything in this book, with some "wireframe" lines of action and a loose filling in of body mass.

These figures need to overlap with the octopus. If they don't, they will look rather

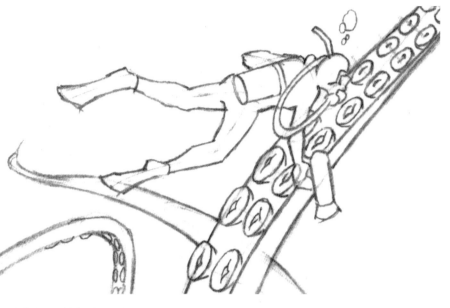

## 7: FINAL DETAILS —1

This is where we finish off our miniature divers and get some three-dimensionality into our suckers.

Don't put too much detail into your divers. Their primary purpose is to serve as indicators of scale, not to steal the show from the star. A few air bubbles rising from their breathing equipment is good, though.

Now for those suckers. For the larger ones we can use three simple curved lines to indicate the shape of the center of the sucker, as shown in the close-up above. Two more curved lines make the cup shape joining the sucker to the tentacle. As the tentacles decrease in size, so should the detail we put into the suckers.

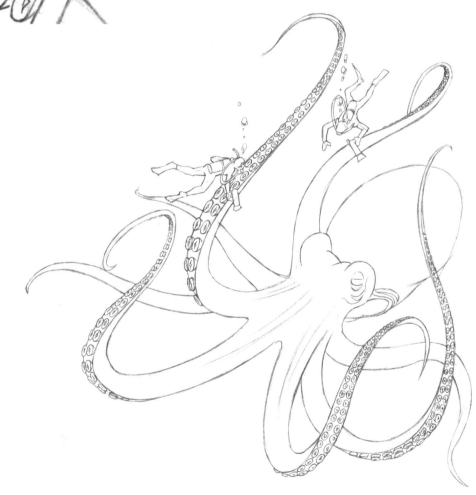

## 7: FINAL DETAILS—2

To finish up, we'll put the final touches to the body of our octopus.

The outer surface of the mantle is made up of loose bumps. Try to imagine the skin of a dragon but make it much looser and softer. As they work their way around the shape of the mantle they come closer together and more numerous.

Small circular bumps now run along the lines we drew back on page 84. Add a few more slightly larger ones between the eyes and you're all done.

# CENTAUR

The centaur has its origins in the Greek myths and is a composite creature: half-man, half-horse.

Male centaurs are notoriously filled with machismo, their favorite pursuits include hunting, fighting and swilling wine. One of Hercules' best friends was a Centaur.

## 1: LINE OF ACTION

We're going to draw our centaur both rearing up on its hind legs and preparing to fire an arrow.

Our first few lines need to get the basic idea of this established, so a long, arching curve for the creature's back is the central element here.

We'll also loosely indicate the horse's legs and the human arm that will hold the bow. If you look at the arm and the two legs nearest us you'll see their spacing and angles follow the line of the body like the hands of a clock at six, half-past seven and nine o'clock respectively. This pattern gives the pose a lot of strength.

## 2: MAJOR BODY PARTS

Unusually, we have to deal with two different bodies when drawing centaurs. Getting this to look perfectly natural isn't easy. By making sure both the horse's body and the human torso conform to our original

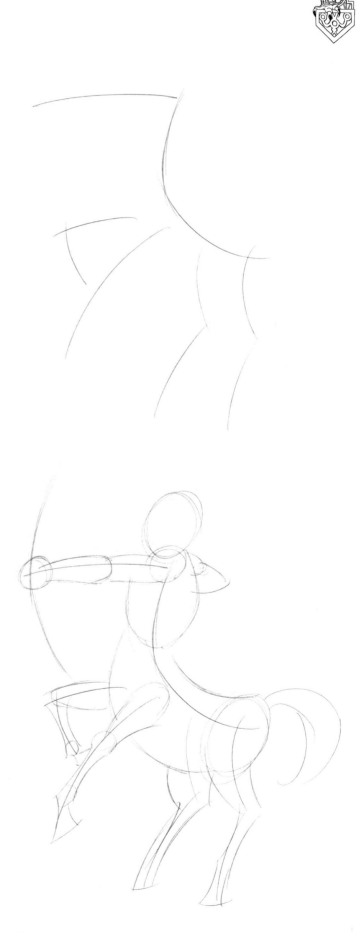

arching curve we can achieve a believable join.

There are six limbs to deal with here, arranged in three pairs. Their positions are largely determined by their functions. The hind legs support the entire weight of the centaur and must look balanced. The forelegs are free to do as they please, so we'll use them to make an expressive shape. The arm holding the bow needs to be dead straight, telling the viewer that the arm is locked at the elbow.

Oh, and don't forget to give your centaur a head!

### 3: MINOR BODY PARTS—1

Our centaur's head is at roughly a three-quarter angle to the viewer so let's start by putting in a curved line dividing his face in two. We can now put in some guidelines for his eyes, nose

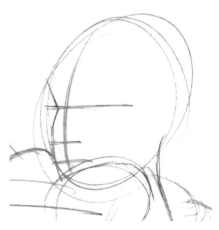

and mouth. Notice that in this position the centaur's chin will be hidden behind his shoulder. The last part of the basic face structure is the divot on the left side of his head indicating his cheek and eye socket.

Staying in that area for a moment, roughly indicate the position of the hand pulling back the drawstring. This should be adjacent to his chin.

For the other hand, indicate the position of the knuckles. These should loosely follow the shape of the bow, which has now been made more substantial.

Let's get some more substance into those hooves. I'm not at all sure if a centaur would favor wearing horseshoes, but I've indicated them anyway.

Lastly, roughly put in the drawstring and arrow.

74

## 4: MINOR BODY PARTS -2

Being the rough, burly types they are, centaurs favor having a full beard and a good mop of hair. This needn't be fussy or detailed.

Put the upper eyelid in at our original guideline, then the lower eyelid. Then put the pupil in between them. Top this off with a strong, determined eyebrow.

Now for his nose. We already have the location of both the bridge and the bottom of the nose from our guidelines so it should be a straightforward task to put this in.

We'll also start to look at the muscles on his torso. There's a large muscle called the latissimus dorsi that runs from the armpit to the small of the back in a gentle "S" shape. His chest muscles, or "pecs" also run from the armpit towards the center of his torso. Indicate his

stomach muscles, or "abs" as shown too.

Work out the shape of the arrowhead and the flight at the other end. The point at which

LATISSIMUS
DORSI

the drawstring, thumb and flight come together needs to be worked out so that the string is in the notch of the flight while the thumb holds this in place.

Let's begin to work some more form into the legs at this point as well, particularly at the joints.

## 5: CLEAN UP

Now would be a good time to get the eraser and a freshly sharpened pencil out before we put the final muscles in.

## 6: FINAL DETAILS—1

If you're not very familiar with human anatomy, the arm muscles we need to put in here may prove difficult. The best way to proceed is to put the elbow in first as most muscles flow in and out of this point.

For the first time in this book I'm going to get the ruler out. The reason for this is that our arrow has to be dead straight. It's a good idea to avoid using rulers except for when drawing man-made objects that obviously benefit from a ruler's perfect edge.

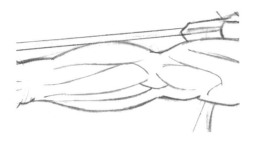

The muscles of the other arm are much simpler with just a hint of the triceps being indicated.

The small group of muscles in front of the *latissimus dorsi* are called the *serratus* muscles and follow the ribs.

We should put some more hairs into our centaur's tail too. Notice that rather than being drawn straight they twist as they flow out of the rump, helping to add life.

SERRATUS MUSCLES

## 7: FINAL DETAILS—2

Finish off by adding some shadowing. Up until now I've avoided doing this in order to leave it up to you as to whether you wish to finish off in pencils or inks. For some examples of this check out the final few pages.

We've lit our centaur simply with light directly from above, casting a shadow on to the ground below. This has the effect of "sticking" the subject to the ground.

Cross-hatching has been used for most of the shadowing on the body.

# WEREWOLF

No book of mythical creatures would be complete without at least one transforming creature: one that changes with the advent of some outside phenomenon.

In the case of the werewolf it's the coming of the full moon that causes an ordinary person to mutate into a crazed, bloodthirsty carnivore!

## 1: LINES OF ACTION

Our werewolf is going to be depicted in a running pose. One way to help give the impression of running is to use an off-balance pose. Our werewolf couldn't possibly be stationary in this position. Provided we get the balance of the limbs right we'll produce a convincing figure.

The shoulders and pelvis are at a similarly tilted angle.

## 2: MAJOR BODY PARTS

Once we have the position of the shoulders organized we can then draw the triangular shape of the torso. Use two lines connecting with the pelvis line.

If the right leg is forward then the left arm should be forward and vice-versa. This is a basic rule for all figures when running or walking.

We need to place the head almost halfway down the shoulder line. Necks are nearly always brought forward when drawing running figures.

Flesh out the legs in line with the guides and use some loose ovals just to indicate the position of the feet.

### 3: MINOR BODY PARTS—1

We can use the original central line of action as the dividing line for the face. Place the eyes and nose above and below the shoulder line as shown. Use two inward curving lines to establish the shape of the werewolf's jaws, down from the shoulder line towards the chest.

The arms for now are put in using simple, elongated ovals.

Having already put in the eyes and nose, placing the ears should be straightforward. They are essentially simple, curved triangles. Don't make them too symmetrical, though.

The fingers and thumbs are drawn in the most basic way for the moment. Remember, the task at this point is only to establish the positions and rough shape of the body parts, not to produce any kind of finished artwork.

You may have noticed a curved line running behind the head and between the shoulders. This is the area where the top of the back meets the neck.

The last line to place at this stage is the upward curve at the belly area. This is a very important line as it tells us a lot about the angle of the torso as the werewolf runs towards us. This curve represents the belt line of our werewolf's ripped trousers. Together with the low shoulders we now have the basics of what we need to demonstrate the dipped position of the werewolf's upper body.

TOP OF BACK

## 4: MINOR BODY PARTS—2

Let's start this stage by finishing off the major facial features.

The "W" shape above the eyes serve as eyebrows, giving our werewolf a very determined expression. From these and at the insides of the eyes we can form the shape of the muzzle, joining the nose with two inswinging curves.

From here we should put in the two nostrils and then form the upper lip from the center line in another gentler "W" shape.

A quick, unfussy curve indicates the lower lip.

Two new lines separate the outside of the ears from the inside, making them very dog-like.

Add a couple of expressive lines around the eyes and begin to show the fur around the neck.

On the body we've placed the chest muscles and six abdominal muscles. The collar bone runs from the top of the chest towards the shoulders.

We'll also make a start on the basic muscles of the arms and shoulders.

Indicate the position of the joints of the fingers and generally firm up the shape of the hands and feet.

## 5: CLEAN UP

Use your eraser to get rid of the
now unnecessary guidelines and
touch up with a sharp pencil.

## 6: MINOR DETAIL—1

Work on finishing up the upper
body. Add some smaller muscle
lines to the shoulders, arms and
at the sides of the torso.

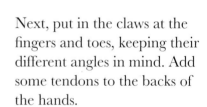

Next, put in the claws at the
fingers and toes, keeping their
different angles in mind. Add
some tendons to the backs of
the hands.

Finish off the jaw area and put
some simple, sharp teeth into
our werewolf's head.

Add some more fur to the top
and sides of the head and work
on getting the shoulders and
forearms looking far more hairy
as well.

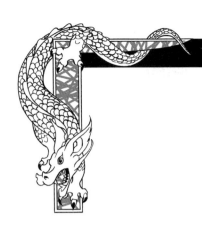

## 7: FINAL DETAILS— 2

The last main thing to attend to is the clothing. We're going to add the shredded remains of a ripped shirt to his torso.

What's left of the shirt loosely follows the shape of our werewolf's chest and shoulders. It bunches and twists at the bottom. Use quick flicks of the pencil to produce the frayed edges of the rest of the shirt.

Add another curved line parallel with the original belt line and add the belt loops around the waistline. Put the long seam in that runs down the werewolf's right leg. As you draw in the pocket, add a couple of kinks where the material wrinkles. Put in the two zipper lines and add the button.

To put a rip into the right knee of the trousers draw a rough hole and then surround this with a series of outward facing curves. Finish this area with a little detail of the now exposed knee.

Fray the bottoms of the trouser leg with a few quick, curved strokes.

To finish off the face, darken a few small areas, noticeably the nose and the areas around the eyes.

# UNICORN

The original visualization of this classic mythical creature was quite different to its currently accepted form. Earliest versions of the creature have it as a cloven-hoofed animal with a billy goat beard. This makes more sense for a horned beast, as only cloven-hoofed animals have this appendage.

While most mythical creatures have their origins in human fears, the unicorn is one of the few exceptions to this, being no threat to humankind. Its horn is said to contain magical anti-toxic qualities and in mythology has been used to neutralize the effects of poisons.

Instead of appearing in Greek mythology the unicorn is instead found in Greek natural history. The Ancient Greeks were quite sure this creature was no myth but rather located in India, a place which for the Greeks was home to a plethora of exotic creatures.

The modern version of the unicorn tends to be a slender white horse with a long, spiralling horn. This is the version we are going to be depicting here.

## 1: LINES OF ACTION

The first things we have to establish are the shape of the body, neck and legs. We want to depict our unicorn in a quite submissive, head down position that will show off its horn.

The best place to start would be with the belly and then loosely indicate the line of the back.

The legs should be both balanced and relaxed. Most of the weight needs to rest on two of the unicorn's legs with the remaining two being slightly raised and bent.

The neck and tail both curve down at approximately 90 degrees, contributing to the relaxed pose.

83

## 2: MAJOR BODY PARTS

Start with the head, using a rough circle shape to indicate the main mass. From here, use a couple of gently curving lines

somewhat foreshortened. The more an object is foreshortened the more extreme the curve becomes.

As we already have guidelines for the legs we can start by putting in the joints at the knees and ankles. Use small, loose

complex and are really made from two sections. We should draw them to integrate with the body.

We also need to fill in the area between the front legs. This can be done with a simple curve for now.

to establish the unicorn's muzzle area. These lines follow the original guideline.

From here we can flesh out the neck and upper back, being sure to put a pronounced curve into the neck. The unicorn's position will cause the neck to be

circle shapes for these. Then roughly show the shapes of the hooves.

We can then use inward curving lines to form the lower legs. The front legs we can form with elongated ovals. The thighs of the hind legs are a little more

Finally, establish the shape of the tail with a few quick flicks of the pencil. This should be much the same shape as the tip of a paintbrush.

## 3: MINOR BODY PARTS

Start by putting in the unicorn's horn. Like the neck, this is partially foreshortened. The viewer is helped in "reading" the angle by the curved line at the horn's base.

Put in two nostrils, noting that the curve of the nose makes the right-hand nostril far more visible.

We can now start on the mane, much of which is falling on the side turned away from us. It very loosely follows the neckline.

Begin to firm up the legs at this stage too, as we need to clean up the drawing soon.

Lastly, add a few fronds at the tip of the unicorn's tail.

We'll put the ears in next, using a couple of narrow triangles.

The lines forming the tops of the eyes need to be part of the same arc and distributed evenly either side of the center line.

When it reaches the ears, part of the mane falls between them and then continues either side of the horn.

Put a thick section of mane at the left-hand side of the unicorn's head.

4: CLEAN UP

Get rid of any now redundant guidelines with an eraser and retouch with a sharp pencil.

5: FINAL DETAILS—1

As should be obvious from the picture below, we're going to work primarily on the mane and tail at this stage.

Along the neck the mane should curl out of the neckline and away from the body. Just above the head, the mane begins to fall over and around the face.

Both the tail and the mane are subdivided into smaller strands that help form their shape.

We'll also finish off the area between the front legs being careful to make these curves

## 6: FINAL DETAILS—2

We need to get the spiral on the horn working. To do this use several angled curves. Try to imagine that the horn is transparent and 'follow' the line

of the creature facing away from the sun will be in shadow.

If we use directional lines that follow the contours of the unicorn's body this will help in giving it form and substance.

conform with the shape of the legs.

There's also a gentle "S" shaped curve used to show the shape of the front of the neck and a muscle line on the upper section of the nearest front leg.

around until it reappears at the front. This will make sure our spiral makes visual sense. Finish by adding some shadows, also using curved lines.

Finish off the unicorn by adding some simple lighting. Any part

The light shadowing lines at the neck are kept deliberately loose and should be done quickly with minimum fuss.

# phoenix

The phoenix is another mythical creature that appears, with variations, in different cultures worldwide. It is probably the boldest representation of the idea of regeneration in all of mythology.

As it nears the end of its life, the phoenix will build a small bonfire made from cinnamon twigs which it then sets alight, burning itself to ashes. From these ashes comes a new, young phoenix.

Being concerned with death and rebirth, it should come as no surprise that the major source of the legend comes from Ancient Egypt. The bird is featured in the Egyptian book of the dead and is seen to represent the setting and rising of the sun.

## 1: LINES OF ACTION

The single most important thing to capture with our first few lines is the upward "sweep" of the bird as it flies out of the fire. The first line we should lay down is the central one forming the "backbone" of the body. From this we can form all the other major shapes, in line with this first curve.

The head, represented by a loose circle is quite small in relation to the body and wings.

The phoenix is generally considered to be a fairly large bird. A smaller bird would have a bigger head relative to the size of its body.

The body of the phoenix is basically pear-shaped, but the front is formed with one line with the back formed with two opposing curves.

The wings are a tilted mirror-image with the right-hand wing facing us and the left-hand wing being at a more oblique angle.

Perspective makes the right-hand wing appear slightly above the left-hand wing.

88

## 2: MAJOR BODY PARTS

We need to divide the wings into two sections. The sections on the inside indicate the flesh-and-bones section of the birds wings which contain smaller, more compact feathers.

The outer sections show the limits of the larger, longer feathers.

We should establish the shape and position of the beak. Two roughly "V" shaped marks join at the bottom and hook over at the top to form the phoenix's bird of prey type beak.

Locate the eye at the top of the head, roughly in the shape of a diamond.

Behind the head we'll establish the limits of what will be the phoenix's decorative feathers.

Use two quick curved lines to create the outlines of the tail feathers and finish them with a few, quick strokes to suggest the individual feathers at the end of the tail.

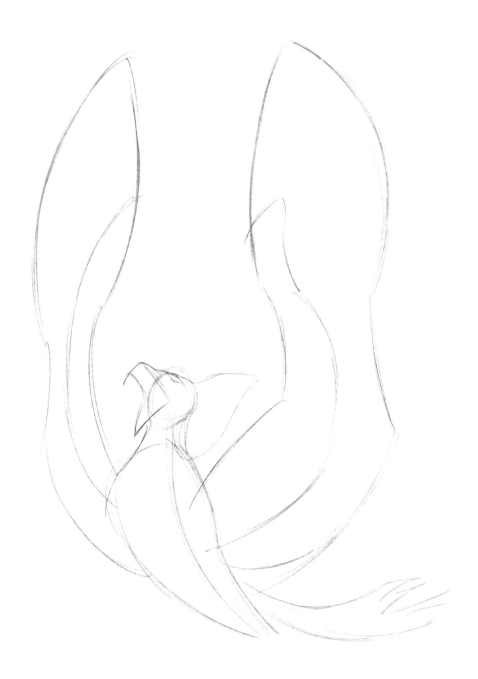

## 3: MINOR BODY PARTS—1

This is where we use the guidelines to add the outer feathers of our phoenix's wings. As you can see, they're at their longest, broadest and loosest at the wing tips, with the remaining feathers being much smaller and tighter.

Again, you should try to use quick strokes to draw these feathers. The trick is to make sure our drawing hand is in the right position to produce the kind of curve we're looking for. We can make sure this is the case by testing the curve before we put pencil to paper. Just keep the pencil tip a couple of millimeters above the paper and check it.

We also need to notice that all of the feathers overlap on the same side as the adjacent feather.

If we get all of this right, we should produce an evenly rendered set of outer feathers, but which retain a lively looseness about them.

We'll also work on the head feathers which should fan around the back of the bird's head. Notice that there are a couple of feathers visible on the other side of the head, too.

We can also work on the beak at this point as well, adding definition to the "hook" part and adding some dimension to the lower half of the beak.

## 4: MINOR BODY PARTS—2

Before we add all of the smaller feathers, we'll need to do a little planning. The lines running along the wings and across the breast represent the areas inside which the smaller feathers will be placed.

I've drawn these guidelines more heavily than I normally would for the sake of clarity. When you draw yours, you should only make then as dark as you need to see them as you put in the smaller feathers.

We also need to place a tongue inside the beak. This is just three lines: one curve for the top and two for the underneath so that the tongue connects at the back and base of our phoenix's mouth.

The tail feathers need to be worked on some more at this point, starting quite tight at the point where the tail joins the body. From here, the tail splays out as the feathers separate from each other.

## 5: CLEAN UP

Erase all of the guidelines with
the exception of those on the
inside of the wings.

## 6: FINAL DETAILS—1

There's one obvious thing that
our phoenix picture is lacking
and that's a fire.

To remain consistent with the
design, the bulk of these flames
have been drawn in roughly the
same direction as the emerging
phoenix.

Those flames at the forefront
are larger than those behind the
phoenix. This helps to add some
depth to our image.

## 7: FINAL DETAILS—2

To finish up we need to add the smaller feathers on the wings and breast.

The smallest feathers are those that run along the ridge at the tops of the wings. These should become larger as they move down the wing towards the larger, looser feathers on the outside of the wings.

The angle at which they're drawn should also curve around with the shape of the wing.

A little above halfway up the wing there's a group of feathers that are a little different. These are smaller, looser and less organized. They represent the end of the flesh and bones part of the wings.

We just need to put in a few feathers on the breast and a row of feathers around the throat. Above this, add a few feathers to the throat.

Darken the inside of the upper beak with a few small lines. These should follow the shape of the beak.

Add the extra delineation around the eye area and put in a nostril and you're done.

# SEA MONSTER

Tales of huge, unidentified species of sea-beast have been spun by mariners for just about as long as man has been sailing the oceans.

Some of these have later been demonstrated to be merely whales or large sharks, while others have remained mysteries unexplained by any known species.

Our serpentine monster is going to be big enough to swallow a small launch.

## 1: LINE OF ACTION

I said "serpentine," so it's only fitting that our first line that goes down should be a quickly whipped-up backwards "S" shape. This gives us a good, dynamic shape to hang our monster's body on.

## 2: MAJOR BODY PARTS

Our monster will be a simple creature, without limbs. A little like a giant eel from Hell.

As our sea monster will be suddenly emerging from the ocean, we needn't worry about the back end of its body for now. But the part of its body that is out of the water needs to be slightly fatter at its middle, narrowing towards the head

and widening slightly where the head joins the neck.

For the monster's head, quickly define an oval roughly in line with the angle of the body.

94

## 3: MINOR BODY PARTS—1

The first thing we need to establish at this stage is the large eye. This is roughly circular and is placed around two-thirds of the way up the monster's head.

What our sea monster lacks in limbs it makes up for in appendages. We'll give him a pair of antennae and some whiskers. We'll also add a long sail-like fin along its back. This line will be our guide for the extent of the monster's spines.

We can't have a sea monster without a sea, so we need to show that our creature is almost leaping out of the water. This is achieved by making it appear as if the monster is "pulling" the water up around it as it erupts out of the ocean. As the water would otherwise be flat, we simply have to draw some curves which join the flat ocean around the monster to the sides of its emerging body.

At the top of this "wave" the creature is creating, we need to show the water breaking up, not unlike a large, violent wave crashing against the rocks. Some extra spray can be added to it later, but for now just use some quickly drawn curves to show the basic effect.

Towards the top of the monster the water that remains is now dripping off its body in large ropes. These ropes will change shape as the creature moves its

body. As a result, they have a gentle "S" shape to them.

The mouth should be wide open so we can show off the monster's teeth.

4: MINOR BODY PARTS—2

Let's get the basic spines of the creature's long dorsal fin in. These follow a roughly 45-degree angle as they curve around the sharp angle of the back.

Next, we'll put the pupil of the eye in, slightly lower than central as we want the monster to be looking downwards.

Use the guides to form the outlines of the whiskers and antennae.

Now for the teeth. We need nasty, pin-sharp teeth for our monster. These should follow the basic jaw line on both upper and lower jaws.

Form some fishy lips with simple parallel lines around the existing mouth outline.

## 5: FINAL DETAILS — 1

Our water needs some more "splash" so let's work on that. Starting with the explosion of water at the monster's base, add a handful of droplets breaking off from the tips of the wave. If we make their shape loosely follow the angle of the wave they'll make better visual sense and have more impact.

We've added some more water and splashes around the head too, using the same principles. Have some flying off those antennae for good measure. More water break-up on the actual body of the monster would be good as well. We can also make the ropes "drippier" too.

On the head, we've added some gums for the teeth to sit in. We've also put in a tongue using a central dividing line to give it shape.

Now to finish the spines. These are wide at their bases, tapering to sharp points at their tips. Join them all up near their tips using "U" shaped curves which should follow the original outer guideline.

as over-the-top as you like, or just confine the effect to specific areas.

On the creature's body the main addition here is the use of shading.

Put in two small areas on the pupil to leave white and fill the rest in. This will create light reflections in the eye's pupil.

Get the inside of the mouth good and dark to get some depth to the features and shadow any remaining areas as you see fit.

## 6: CLEAN UP

There are plenty of guidelines which are now redundant to erase before finishing up, so get that eraser out and then touch up where necessary.

## 7: FINAL DETAILS—2

Let's get that water really whipped up by the use of some speed lines at the base of our monster. These have to be put down quickly to be really effective. They should be aimed roughly at the points where the water is breaking up around the creature.

Next, firm up the dripping areas, adding as many extra droplets and splashes as you feel the image needs. You can go

# CHIMERA

The word *chimera* or *chimerical* can be applied to any creature which is made up from two or more different animals.

In ancient Greek mythology the Chimera was part lion and part goat with a tail made of snakes. It could breathe fire and was the offspring of Typhon and Echidna. It was slain by the hero Bellerophon with the aid of the winged horse Pegasus.

## 1: LINES OF ACTION

We first need to establish the basic pose. For this we want our chimera to be adopting a strong upright pose. Use a curved line as the foundation of an arched back and put its legs and arms apart, as above.

## 2: MAJOR BODY PARTS

Let's start with the torso and give our creature a deep chest represented by a large oval.

The goat part of the chimera will have a long neck, the lion a much thicker and shorter one. Having put in the tapering curves of the neck we can add the two heads. These are quite different shapes. For now, they are roughly an oval and a circle.

Next, use ovals to construct the rough shape of the arms over the original guidelines. Finish these off with a couple of ovals representing the hands/paws.

The thighs can be roughed out using ovals as well. Remember that they should form the buttocks at the point where they meet, below the tail.

3: MINOR BODY PARTS—1

Now we need to work out the position and shape of the two snakes making up the tail. These should swing out in either direction in order to confront

We'll make a start on the shapes of our chimera's heads. They'll both have open mouths, with the goat partly facing away from us and the lion being shown in profile.

The positions of the joints have already been established by the original lines, so just indicate

these with small circles and use ovals to show the size and position of the feet. Join the feet and knee joints with inward curves.

whatever enemy the chimera is faced with. As our creature is standing at a three-quarter angle to us. The snakes will be forming quite different shapes, as the angles we are viewing them at are quite different.

The curves in the horns won't be similar either. They come out of the head at different angles plus we're viewing them tilted back and at a three-quarter angle.

This can make it very difficult to work out and is usually done with a combination of careful thought and trial and error.

4: MINOR BODY PARTS—2

Let's get the meat of our snakes' bodies into place by following our original guidelines. We can also roughly put in their jaws too.

Our goat's eye is made from two curves in the same direction, due to the angle we are viewing it from. The lion's eye is more straightforward and a simple circle will do for now.

Throw in a few fronds of the lion's mane and we're ready to move on.

We'll carry on putting in the facial features of the lion and goat. The goats ears should be a little floppy while the lion's should be smaller and upright.

The goat's horns follow the guidelines coming out of the head into a steady taper as they make their way towards the fairly sharp tips.

## 5: MINOR BODY PARTS—3

We need to start building up some of the muscle structure of our beast.

shape. Either side of the top of this "S" we can place the shoulder blades. At the base of the spine we can add some spinal muscle parallel with the spine line.

anatomy. There is insufficient room available in this book to share much about it here but as a guide the muscle lines are not parallel with each other but rather form less predictable shapes as they travel down the

This will add both substance and believability to our chimera.

First, we should form the basis of the spine with a gentle "S"

We need to add some muscle to the lion's arm as well. As with the centaur on page 92 this can be difficult if we don't know something about

arm from the elbow to the wrist. We'll also add some tendons at the ankles, as well as some claws to both the front and hind paws.

Indicate the tongues of the snakes and add a couple of eyes.

Both heads of our chimera still require some more work. On the lion's face we've added some lines indicating the cheeks and a

Lastly for the lion we'll give him some big, nasty teeth in the top and bottom jaws and put in a curved triangle for his nose.

Let's add a little fur to the neck of the goat and a little at the

6: CLEAN UP

Our drawing is now sufficiently messy to warrant getting the eraser out for a tidying up session. As always, touch up any resulting weak spots with a

couple of wrinkles at the bridge of the nose. This helps with the snarling expression. More shape needs to be given to the ears and the outline of the mane needs finishing.

elbow. Then we'll firm up the goat's mouth area, putting in a line to indicate the teeth of the lower jaw.

well sharpened pencil and we're ready for the final details.

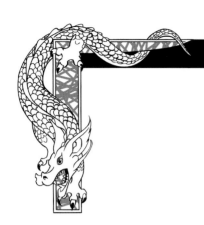

## 7: FINAL DETAILS—1

We now need to get into the surface detail, specifically on

of the snake while the left-hand one is more decorative.

If you've been working your way through this book you should by now be able to visualize the shape of these

and then using these guides to contour the snakes' bodies with them.

The other thing we need to attend to here are the ridges on the goat's horns. These

those snakes. We're going to give them both different patterns, mainly because we can. The right-hand pattern is great for showing off the shape

snakes in your mind before you put the patterns down. It should simply be a question of marking off sections representing the occurrence of each pattern

too should wrap around the shape of the horns, but not too exactly. If we're too exact the effect will be unnatural.

## 8: FINAL DETAILS — 2

To finish our chimera off we now need to add some more body to the lion's mane. If we put more emphasis on the mane's underneath this will give it some real shape. A little more detail at the inside of the lion's ear needs to be added, too.

We'll also put some cross-hatching work on the underside of both snakes to help bring their shape out further.

Finally, add some last detail at the backs of the legs and we're almost there......

105

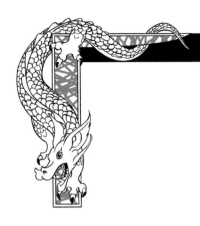

## 9: FINAL DETAILS—3

To really bring out the shape of our chimera we should add some lighting effects.

With the figure lit by sunlight directly from above, any parts of the body which are hidden from the sun have been shaded. Some extra fur has been added to the goat's neck and the undersides of the ears, as well as on some smaller areas of both faces.

106

# GRIFFIN

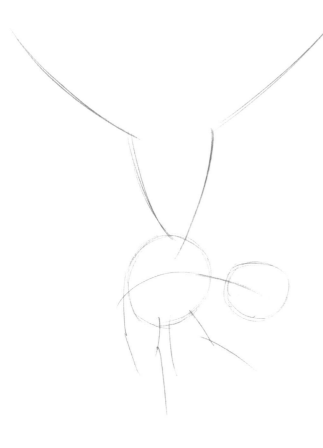

front legs will be much further forward as we're going to put the hind legs on top of a rock.

The wings are close to symmetrical, so a couple of quick, unfussy lines can be used to represent these.

## 2: MAJOR BODY PARTS

We can start by joining the body and head by using two inward curving lines to make the neck.

The thighs can be put in using basic oval shapes and the lower legs use inward curves to form their shape. Sketch in the rough shape of the talons with simple, curved lines.

The griffin, or gryphon, is another composite beast, having the body of a lion and the wings, head and talons of an eagle.

The griffin's origins go back many millennia to the ancient Middle and Near East: Babylonia, Persia and Assyria as well as ancient Egypt.

## 1: LINES OF ACTION

We want to show our griffin in an aggressive posture with its wings raised. Let's start with a circle representing the griffin's body and work outwards. A curved line represents the foreshortened aspect of the body, neck and head. The

The eagle's beak has a much larger upper bill and can be roughed in with just a couple of curves for now.

We'll form the "S" shape of the tail in one go as there's no great need for guidelines on this.

3: MINOR BODY PARTS—1

Let's get some detail into the griffin's head. As usual start with the eye to orient ourselves,

crooked shape to the underside of the top part of the beak and the hook should come down at approximately 90 degrees.

There are two things we need to do with the wings at this stage: Firstly, divide them into two sections with the lines shown, much as we did with the phoenix. Secondly, create the four "leading" feathers, those at the tips of the wings with some quick, simple curves.

Having roughly established the direction of the talons, we can put in their pads, those parts of the foot from which the talons emanate.

The griffin needs a "brush" at the end of its tail. As this is essentially a male lion's tail it should be the shape of a big, thick watercolor brush tip.

The wings are similar to others found in this book. We need to make sure they are firmly rooted to the creature's back and are almost identical in shape and size.

putting in a pupil and an expressive line above the eye. Fill in the ears and the details that separate the beak from the rest of the face. There's a

## 4: MINOR BODY PARTS — 2

We want our griffin to look at home, so we're going to mount him on a rock, of the kind found in the griffin's natural habitat, a cliff face.

We can make the rock any shape we choose, just as long as the top and bottom are located in the right place in consideration of the griffin's pose.

Next comes the first, outer row of feathers. We've already done something very similar with the phoenix, just make sure that the angles of the feathers follow the guideline and don't make them too perfect.

Let's get some more detail into the face, too. We'll double up the outline of the mouth to form a lip area around the beak. Next we'll put in the nostril about halfway up the upper beak and

join the lip up with this, then continue this line over the top of the beak. Put in the fold of skin at the corner of the mouth. Add the tongue then draw the lip on the other side of the mouth. Darken the tip of the beak and the area under the tongue.

We can now add the talons, making sure they are in line with the direction of the pads we drew in the last stage.

## 5: CLEAN UP

Let's consolidate what we've got, erasing the guidelines we no longer need.

## 6: FINAL DETAILS—1

Our griffin has a great deal of detail, so we'll take these last stages slowly.

Start by adding a row of small feathers running along the "arms" of the wings. From there, add more rows, making the feathers grow in size as you move towards the outer row.

"V" shaped lines to these to be filled in later.

The tips of the leading feathers have also been marked off for darkening using "V" shaped lines.

FEATHER SHAFTS

Rather than follow strict guidelines for the insides of the wings as we did with the phoenix, we'll use a looser approach here.

This way we get a much less mathematical and more organic arrangement of our feathers. The outer row are going to have darker tips, so we'll add some

Leave them like this until we add the shading in stage 8.

Finally, we need to add the shafts of the feathers, shown

as two tapering lines leading towards the tips of the larger feathers.

## 7: FINAL DETAILS—2

feathers being found at the griffin's cheeks. The feathers should go back as far as the point where the neck meets the body. We can also vary the curves at the feathers' edges

Down the front of the legs and down almost to the talons run a series of hexagonal shapes. These should flatten out as they move from the leg to the talon.

Now we'll concentrate on the head feathers and the skin of the griffin's lower legs.

We can use narrow and wide feathers to help show the shape of the head with the widest

according to their placing on the head. As with the wings, try to make sure your feathers aren't so uniform as to rob them of life and believability.

If we repeat this pattern for the other talons we build up a honeycomb type of pattern. This is both decorative and practical as it helps to visually describe the shapes of the legs.

## 8: FINAL DETAILS—3

The shading of the feathers and the addition of more lion fur to bring out the shape of the body is all that remains to be done.

We need to keep our pencil sharp and use quick strokes of the pencil to achieve a good, feathery effect.

Firm up the shape of the rock and add the shadow cast by the griffin.

We're done.

# MEDUSA

The Medusa was one of the Gorgons of Greek legend. Her hair was made of snakes and she had the power to turn a person to stone, should they have the misfortune to gaze upon her face.

It was Perseus who finally brought her reign of terror to an end. He achieved this with the aid of a reflective shield, allowing him to see the Medusa without looking at her directly.

This is probably the toughest drawing in this book. It's certainly the most detailed which is why I've saved it until now. To do it properly requires a lot of patience and planning but is a very rewarding image if we follow the steps carefully.

## 1: LINES OF ACTION

This is a more complex initial drawing than usual. With a drawing this detailed we need to get up to speed quickly.

The central, curved line in the image above represents the angle of the body and neck. To this, add the oval that represents Medusa's head.

Crossing this is another curved line representing the collar bone which connects the shoulders.

The arm is foreshortened, so the curve of its line will be quite strong. Add an oval for the position of the hand.

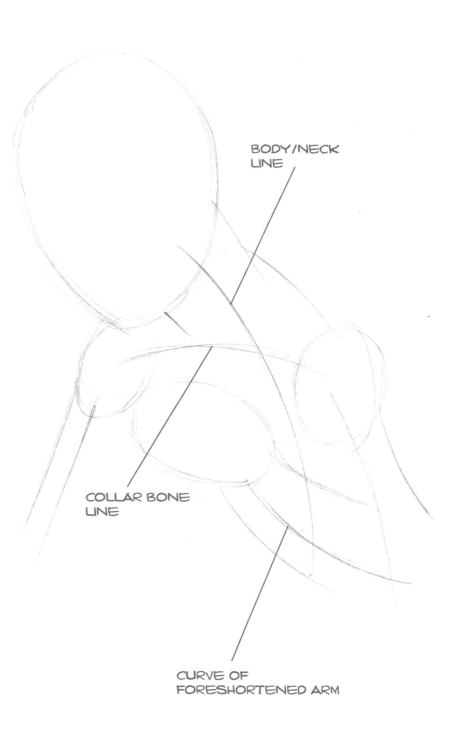

BODY/NECK LINE

COLLAR BONE LINE

CURVE OF FORESHORTENED ARM

## 2: MAJOR BODY PARTS—1

Start with the face, creating a curved center line. Through this place guidelines for the eyes, nose and mouth.

We'll then begin to work out the shapes of the snakes, concentrating for now just on the ones at the front. We want to ultimately create a twisting, writhing mass of them, so it's important to use lively looking shapes whilst at the same time trying not to lose control of what we're trying to achieve.

## 3: MAJOR BODY PARTS—2

Using the top of the oval representing the hand as a guide, put in the knuckles on the bony hand reaching out for us. From these knuckles we can draw guidelines for the fingers using three lines. We then flesh these out to produce the rough outlines of the fingers.

Place the thumb at the left-hand side of the oval, behind the fingers.

Put in the eye sockets along the guidelines then add a circle for the tip of the nose.

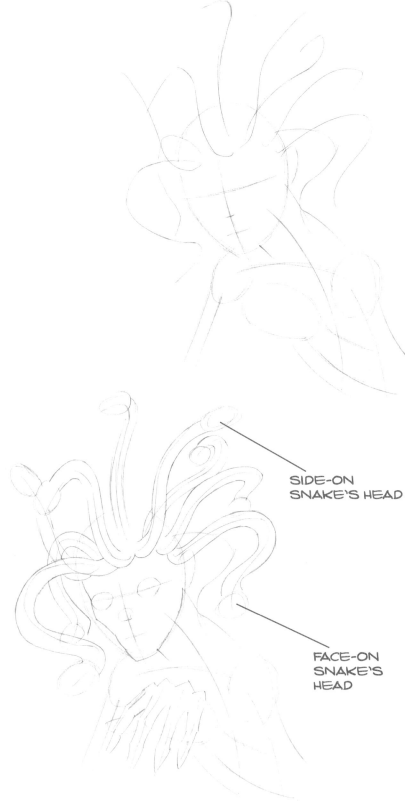

SIDE-ON SNAKE'S HEAD

FACE-ON SNAKE'S HEAD

Now for those snakes. We first need to make a decision about which snakes are in front of the others and draw their bodies first. Once we've got those fleshed out it's a fairly simple task to put in the others' bodies behind them.

114

The rough shapes we use for the snakes' heads will depend on the angle we've drawn them at. Use ovals for the ones that are going to be viewed side-on and shapes closer to circles for the ones that face us.

The snakes should curl upwards from our Medusa's "hairline" and avoid simply sticking straight out.

## 4: MINOR BODY PARTS—1

With the snakes at the front of Medusa's head now in place we can put in some more guidelines for the next group. Keep the shapes interesting and interacting with each other.

The next stage of building up the face can start with putting in the cheekbone line on the right side of the face. This would follow the line of the skull beneath the skin.

Next, add the eyebrows, eyelids and pupils.

From the left-hand eyebrow draw a curve running down to join the tip of the nose.

Next we need to form the lips. The lower lip is usually slightly thicker than the upper lip. The downwards curve under the lower lip helps to bring out the shape of the chin.

We should start on her clothes here as well. They all loosely follow the shape of her body at

the neck and shoulders. Our Medusa will be wearing a loosely fitting, gathered tunic. For now, simply draw in some areas of cloth at these points and we'll add more detail later. Draw a ring around her neck, to which we'll add a collar later.

Put in some loose curves where the material bunches up at the shoulders.

The palms of her hands also need adding in as well at the point where they join the wrist. Add the basic curves for a sleeve here too.

## 5: MINOR BODY PARTS—2

We need to add the bodies to our latest snakes' guidelines, making sure we get their interactions right. Whatever we draw it all has to make sense, no matter how complex the patterns we build up.

When we're happy with the body shapes we can make a start on a few of our snakes heads. The two most prominent ones at the front would be good to get established along with one or two others.

Let's put some life into those eyes and establish the nostrils some more.

Add some folds to the fabric around the neck and shoulders and some more folds at the cuffs near her wrist and her elbow.

Next, we'll take the hands to the next level by adding some knuckle guides and fingernails. Add a tendon on the underside of the wrist and delineate the arm bone where it meets the wrist.

It's starting to get very complex and quite messy now. Try to bear with me just a little longer as a few more small additions need to be made before we clean up.

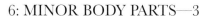

## 6: MINOR BODY PARTS—3

We shouldn't add too much detail to our snakes' faces before we clean up. All we need to do at this point is work out all of the most general features: mainly the eyes and mouths.

We should try to come up with a variety of interesting shapes and positions for the faces of our snakes: mouths fully open, shut or in between.

One last thing: we need to add the detail of the inside of Medusa's ear.

## 7: CLEAN UP

We've pretty much reached the saturation point of what our eyes can practically cope with now.

We really have to put the eraser to work. Do so very carefully though as it will prove difficult to make perfect sense of such a complex collection of lines if we accidentally rub out the meaningful ones.

8: FINAL DETAILS—1

So far our Medusa has been rather more attractive than her reputation, so we need to "ugly" her up a little. Or a lot.

This will be achieved by putting nasty cracks all over her once lovely face. As with previous patterns, we need to have the lines at least loosely follow the shape of the surface they lie on. Use the cracks to describe every undulation that the cracks of the skin travel over.

It's best to leave the eyelids, nose tip and lips alone as they will become lost among the cracks if we include them.

We ought to make a start on the surface of the snakes by drawing the segments of their underbellies. We'll also start to add some more details such as their tongues and teeth.

The folds of skin have been added to Medusa's knuckles. Some reflection lines help bring out the shape of her fingernails.

The eyes have also had some work too. The eyelashes are made from a few quick flicks of the pencil and the corners of the eyelids have been shaded to bring out their shape.

## 9: FINAL DETAILS—2

The technique used to add the scales to the snakes is very similar to the one we used way back in the dragons section. For a reminder, see pages 37, 56 and 63.

Here, we need to scale that technique down and be wary of the complexities caused by the interweaving snakes' bodies.

Try to vary the size and shape of the scales a little from snake to snake as this will help the viewer make better visual sense of the image.

The scales on the snakes' faces need to be handled with a little more care. The scales surrounding the eye tend to form a rough circle. If we draw these first we can then draw the remaining scales coming off this circle and following the shape of the head.

On the nearest, biggest snake, I've used a different pattern, just to break things up a little. We could use what ever patterns we like on these snakes' bodies, just as long as we maintain visual balance in the overall final picture.

Add some more weight to Medusa's eyebrows and some lighting effects on the clothing and Medusa's ear.

10: FINAL DETAILS—3

A little shading work and tightening up puts the finish on our image.

120

# APPENDIX

# FINISHES

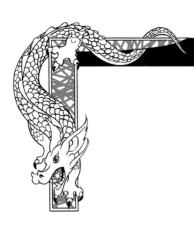

Throughout this book I've kept all the drawings as clean and clear as possible for two reasons. One is to make sure every stage of the drawing is easy to understand. The other is because it's ultimately up to you how you want to complete your drawing.

If we're not going to be adding color to our final images we'll probably want to finish off with some quite involved pencil shading.

If we're intending to scan and color our images with the aid of a computer we'll probably want to finish by inking our drawings. This provides extremely well defined, self-contained areas perfect for filling in with the computer's tools.

I've included several examples of each on these last pages. Their quite radical difference in appearance is due to their ultimate functions as artwork.

Having a clear idea of this is essential for maintaining a focused approach to our work.

The shading on the griffin's wings and body will be added to the inked version, but using color instead of pencil. The approach is much the same, albeit with a far wider variety of choice as to tone and hue.

It requires a lot of careful consideration to get the shadowing right on as complex an image as the Medusa.

It would have been even harder if I'd chosen to light her from the side instead of directly from above; the most straightforward way of lighting a subject.

With the penciled version of the sea monster, shown here to the right, the body is filled in with gray, allowing the water areas on the body to stand out.

The shading also gives the body more substance.

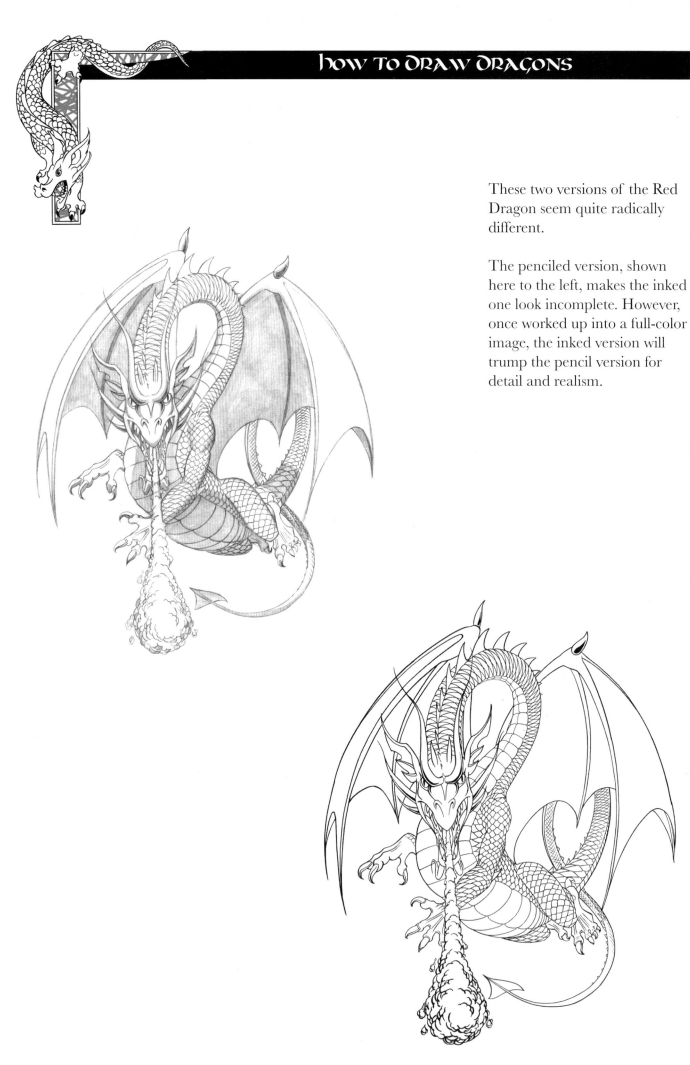

These two versions of the Red Dragon seem quite radically different.

The penciled version, shown here to the left, makes the inked one look incomplete. However, once worked up into a full-color image, the inked version will trump the pencil version for detail and realism.

# GLOSSARY

**Cross-hatching:** a technique using diagonal crossing lines to produce a shading effect. This was first used by engravers to achieve variety of tone when using only black ink.

**Draw through:** this technique is used primarily when working out major body parts. The outlines of the shapes overlap to ensure all of the body parts convincingly work together. Once we're happy all the parts fit together, we erase the lines we no longer need.

**Feathering:** a way of creating soft, graduated lines of shading. This is achieved by using fast strokes of a pencil or pen, usually with the lines parallel and close together.

**Foreshortening:** this term applies to objects when viewed at more extreme angles, particularly head-on. For example, when an arm and hand is rotated 90 degrees from a side view to a position where the hand is closest to our eyes we would use the rules of foreshortening to depict both the change in shape and scale.

**Lines of action:** these are the first, most basic lines we draw when establishing the size and pose of anything we draw. We should try to capture as much of the essence of our subject as possible with these few simple strokes.

**Perspective:** this is the technique of determining the angles of objects as they appear between us and the horizon. It is the most powerful tool for creating convincing looking backgrounds and landscapes.

**Surface form:** we can use the superficial markings, scales, light patterns etc. to help us describe the shape of any object. We do this by understanding how these change with the differing shapes of our subject. To understand this put an interestingly shaped object underneath a single light source such as a lamp. As you move the object around, the shadow will alter as it describes the surface form.

**Wireframe:** a term related to lines of action. Wireframes are usually slightly more complicated versions and represent a greatly simplified skeleton of our subject. Their function is to show the major dynamic aspects of what we are trying to draw. Over this wireframe we can then add the substance of our subject, building in complexity as we go.